L[illegible]

GOLF
IN THE CAPE

WHERE TO PLAY
AND WHERE TO STAY IN
SOUTH AFRICA

LARRY GOULD

for Peggy-

my golfing partner and partner in life.

and

Special thanks to those who allowed me to

play golf

while they did the work!

Claire van Staden

Gillian O'Leary

Herby Wüst

Nick Castle

Gill Wrench

Melanie Vogt

Barbara and Lambert van Rijsewijk

and

A special mention for Juan Espi

who not only provided the splendid golf course photographs

but also proved to be an amiable companion

who regularly asked me why he was

photographing grass!

CONTENTS

First published in Cape Town 1995
Second edition 1996
Third edition 1998
Fourth edition 2000
Larry Gould Publishing

ISBN: 0-620-30064-7

produced by Bay Print
printed in Singapore
design and layout by van Rijsewijk Studio
reproduction by Castle Graphics
map by Big 6 Studio

INTRODUCTION

by Dennis Alpert
Chief Executive of 'The Presidents Cup.'

September 11 resulted in The Presidents Cup being delayed by one year. Out of all bad comes some good, as this allowed my family and I to spend more time in this wonderful part of the world. The Cape is blessed with an abundance of beauty, variety and exceptional people. All of this will no doubt be reflected during The Presidents Cup to be held at Fancourt Hotel and Country Club Estate in George on the Garden Route of South Africa, in November 2003. A worldwide television audience of over 400 million will watch the best golfers of the USA battle the Best of the Rest of the World (excluding Ryder Cup countries) and I have no doubt that Fancourt, the Garden Route and South Africa in particular will capture the hearts of the public.

For those lucky enough to visit the Cape to play golf, there is so much on offer. Larry Gould's guide has set out the best of the choices by describing the golf courses and advising you where to stay in the region. That he is qualified to do this, I can vouch for personally. We have shared a stage presenting the wonders of this country to international tour operators and travel agents. His passion and love for South Africa is contagious. Larry describes himself as "A Frenchman by birth, an Englishman by education and a South African by choice." He was the former General Manager of Fancourt and left this wonderful location to fulfil his dream to promote South Africa as 'one of the world's favoured golf destinations'. For the past eight years Larry has travelled throughout this land, playing and writing about the golf courses and staying in some of the wonderful hospitality establishments this country has on offer. As he puts it "Somebody's got to do it!"

The result is the guide you are reading now. It is full of useful information for the visiting golfer, with some descriptions of holes on each course as well as some glimpses of what is available in the areas around the courses.

For this guide, Larry has chosen 37 of the 18-hole courses and one of the 9-holes, chosen because they are tourist friendly and geographically diverse. This should not detract from the other 18-hole and 9-hole courses, all of which are listed at the back of the guide.

The President's Cup®
2003

The Grea
Golf Event
on the
African Contine

Fancourt - Home of The Presidents Cup

test

nt

THE PRESIDENTS MEN

Gary Player
Captain International Team

Jack Nicklaus
Captain USA Team

THE GOLF TOURIST

This book has been researched and written for you who thoroughly enjoy the game of golf. It was literally designed to suit your pocket-for not only is it inexpensive for the wealth of information it provides, but it does slip easily into your pocket, golf bag or luggage.

It addresses the needs of those of you driving short distances from home to try a new weekend challenge, the businessman staying over in a new environment or the family man and group holiday maker from up country South Africa or further afield in Africa. It is also aimed at the dedicated overseas tourist and those of you essential behind-the-scenes operators, travel agents, golf tour organisers, hoteliers, information centres and golf guides who plan, advise and smooth out the wrinkles to make the game of golf the most enjoyable of games.

This is one of a series of Gould's Guides to Golf. The others are the Guide to Golf in Kwazulu Natal and Mpumalanga and The Guide to Golf in Gauteng and Surrounds.

Each guide is specifically a directory of where to play and where to stay, identifying hotels and guesthouses conveniently located near specific golf courses. Similarly, the hotels chosen are page positioned throughout the guide close to the golf courses described.

Gould's special note

It is important to note that for the greater Cape Metropolitan area the hotels and guest houses listed are ALL within easy distances of ALL the Cape Town courses.

Gould's very special note

The holes described on each golf course do NOT correspond to the photographs shown—these are to give you a broader view of each course prior to your visit!! Metrages are from the club tees, unless otherwise stated.

WHEN TO PLAY

The Cape golf region described in this book sweeps the Southern coastal strip from Cape Town, near the southernmost tip of Africa, to beyond the Great Fish River near East London. For the golfer it is a land blessed with warm dry summers and mild winters with its courses playable all through the year. Winter golf can be a joy. The usual squalls and blustery westerlies tend to last four or five days then give way to calm weather, wind free, with crystal clear days and balmy warm air - the phenomena known locally as "berg wind" conditions. In spring the weather improves, the air is warmer and after the winter rains, the courses reach peak condition.

Mid-summer days are hot and clear. This is also the time of the 'Southeaster', a wind that reaches some velocity, especially in the Western Cape, and will add the necessity of learning to play a low punch shot to enhance your golfing experience. The most perfect golfing circumstances come into play in autumn. Days are warm, sunny and wind free and the courses are usually less crowded.

TRANSPORT

This is a land of big space. The distance from Cape Town to Plettenberg Bay is similar to that of London to St. Andrews, and to East London, a similar distance again. Yet with these vast distances the national roads (N1 and N2) are superb. The surfaces are equivalent to those of international freeways, allowing a constant 120km/h. Regular commercial air services connect Cape Town to George, Port Elizabeth and East London and car rental services are available at the airport with the drop-off zones at any other major centre. Light aircraft at these centres, and on smaller strips, is an alternative choice. Because of the mountains and distances, the railways in this region are not recommended as your prime method of travel, yet the George to Knysna run, by steam train, is one trip to be savoured for its exquisite scenery. Another alternative is the legendary Blue Train that now travels between Cape Town and Port Elizabeth.

Luxury bus services offer a slick schedule with quality air-conditioned comfort along both national routes mentioned.

VALUE FOR MONEY

Since the advent of democracy in 1994, South Africa has enjoyed a rapid growth in its tourist industry. The infrastructure that exists is continually being upgraded to meet the expectations of these new demands. The relatively low visitors fees, added to the tremendously favourable exchange rate with major overseas currencies, is value in itself. Then add the playability of the courses with good weather and long hours of sunshine and you will see this area offers exceptional value. (The story is often told of Japanese visitors who came, bought a full set of clubs from the pro, played, then returned the clubs. They had to be convinced that they had bought the equipment: it wasn't part of the green fees!)

South Africa has in the past been the best kept secret in golf tourism. No longer - we have been discovered. Since you have bought this book, we are happy you have discovered us and we are only too happy to share the knowledge and welcome you. Enjoy your game!

Larry (or Frenchie as I know him) shares my passion for South Africa and its varied golf courses. I can think of no better person to guide you.

Enjoy your visit.

ROYAL CAPE

Royal Cape Golf Course

Length of Course: *5787 metres*

Type of Course: *Parkland*

Holes: *18*

Par: *72*

ROYAL CAPE

Royal Cape Golf Course **Map reference:** *26*
Length of Course: *5787 metres* **Holes:** *18*
Type of Course: *Parkland* **Par:** *72*
Visitors: *Members only on Saturdays and Tuesdays*
Visitors welcome all other days - advisable to book
Club Professional: *Craig Ross 021 761 6552*
Tuition: *Yes* **Club Shop:** *Yes*
Practice Facilities: *Driving range –balls supplied.*
Chipping area, putting green
Hire Facilities: *Clubs, trolleys, caddies and drive carts*
Catering: *Bar, restaurant, halfway house*
Location: *174 Ottery Road, Wynberg, 7800*
Contact: *Dick Lockley*
Postal address: *P.O.Box 186, Ottery 7808*
Phone: *021 761 6551* **Fax:** *021 797 5246*
e-mail: *bookings@royalcapegolf.co.za* **web:** *www.royalcapegolf.co.za*

A ROYAL EXPERIENCE

South Africa's oldest golf club naturally portrays a sense of history and tradition. Improvements to the single storey clubhouse dating back to 1924, have merely served to enhance that sense of tradition and cleverly blend it with the needs of today's golfer. Just stop and look at the honours board and you will see that the South African Championship was first held here in 1910. George Fotheringham won in that year with a score of 315, and again in 1914, with a four round score of 299. The South African Open has been held at this challenging course eleven times since then with notable winners being Gary Player (273) in 1965 and Charles Bolling of the USA (278) in 1983. In 1990, Namibia's Trevor Dodds won with a four round score of 285.The most recent championship (1996) was won by Ernie Els, who tamed the famous layout by posting an eighteen under par total. Established by Lieutenant General Sir Henry D'oyley Torrens in 1885, the club received its 'Royal' title in 1910, following a visit by the Duke of Connaught. The course was originally in the Wynberg area after which it moved to the Rondebosch common in 1890. In 1905, the land on which the course is now located, was acquired.

As one would expect of a Royal Club, this one has moved well with the times. The refurbishment to the clubhouse has been complemented by improvements on the course itself. All 18 greens were re-laid to USGA specifications and planted with dominant bent grass and the result was savoured by the professional golfers competing in the Players Championship, held at the club in 1999, 2000 and 2001. Nic Henning of South Africa won the Championship in 1999 and the budding talent of 21year old Trevor Immelman, also from South Africa, held off the challenge of Ernie Els to win the tournament with a score of 278 in 2000.

In December 2001, Ernie Els fired a last round 65 to overhaul the field with a final score of 273.
The result of these major alterations will serve to provide the visitor with an extremely good year-round golfing experience as well as a comfortable off-course experience, to complement the enjoyable on-course one.
The Royal Cape also has the added attraction of a good practice range situated some distance from the clubhouse.

THE COURSE

The second nine has what the locals call their own 'Amen' corner - two challenging par 3's and a truly magnificent par 4 that are usually played against the prevailing wind!

13th Hole - Par 3 - 158 metres
A testing par 3, made more of a challenge by the southeaster wind. On a calm day front and back bunkers are both in play. Against the wind, the back bunker is rarely reached, as a usual six iron shot becomes a three iron!

14th Hole - Par 4 - 382 metres
This long par 4 curving to the right has water all along the right hand-side, although a severe slice is required for the water to come into play from the tee. However, if the approach to the green is pushed, the water will win! The large green has subtle slopes that make this an added feature to this truly challenging hole.

15th Hole - Par 3 - 137 metres
Once again, this hole features a water hazard. This time, the water runs from the tee to the green and hugs the front right of the green. Front left and back bunkers add to the difficulty and trees, as well as out of bounds on the left, are also cause for concern.

Gould's special note:
The 3rd hole, stroke 1, is one of my favourite par 4's.

THE AREA

From here, you can visit the residential area of Constantia situated along the mountain slopes overlooking Cape Town. Magnificent homes abound in this wealthy area and a visit to Groot Constantia wine estate, where you will find good wines and tradition on offer, should not be missed.
The beautiful Kirstenbosch Botanical Gardens, displaying the richness of the Cape Floral Kingdom, are not far away and are the perfect place to enjoy a stroll, followed by lunch or tea on the restaurant terrace. But, for a quality lunch, you would have to travel far to match the food of Constantia Uitsig, the restaurant in a lovingly restored old Victorian farmhouse set amongst the vineyards on the Tokai road.
Should you be heading back towards the City, it would be worthwhile to make your way back over Constantia Nek via Hout Bay to return along the spectacular coastal road.

CAPE GRACE ★★★★★

V&A WATERFRONT, CAPE TOWN

Surrounded by water on three sides, the luxurious Cape Grace enjoys one of Cape Town's most sought after locations - the West Quay of the Victoria and Alfred Waterfront. The spacious rooms and suites open to unrivalled views with Table Mountain as a majestic backdrop. Winner of the Conde Nast Traveler "Best Hotel in the World" in 2000, the Cape Grace is a member of "The Leading Small Hotels of the World."

General Manager *Tony Romer-Lee.*
121 rooms, swimming pool, library, boardroom, bascule bar, communication centre, ***one.waterfront*** *restaurant. West Quay, Victoria and Alfred Waterfront .*
P.O. Box 51387, Waterfront, Cape Town, 8002.
phone *021 410 7100* **fax** *021 419 7622*
e-mail *reservations@capegrace.com* **website** *www.capegrace.com*

THE CELLARS HOHENORT ★★★★★

CONSTANTIA, CAPE TOWN

The Cellars-Hohenort nestles in the heart of a beautiful suburb of Cape Town. A haven of peace and tranquility unifying two great traditions, the magnificent restoration of the 18th Century Klassenbosch wine cellars and the splendid manor house of the Hohenort. With its understated elegance, the hotel boasts 53 luxury rooms and suites with breathtaking views across the 9 acres of gardens & vineyard. A Relais et Châteaux Hotel.

General Manager *Fredrik Aspegren*
2 restaurants, 2 heated swimming pools, spa, beauty salon, tennis court, golf putting green and gym. 93 Brommersvlei Road, P.O. Box 270, Constantia, 7848.
phone *021 794 2137* **fax** *021 794 2149*
e-mail *cheslyn@cellars-hohenort.co.za* **website** *www.cellars-hohenort.com*

THE MOUNT NELSON HOTEL *****

GARDENS, CAPE TOWN

For over 100 years, The Mount Nelson has been the epitome of grace, excellence, tradition, luxury and a fine retreat in the heart of Cape Town. Recognised as one of the world's finest hotels, this famous landmark continues to provide gracious service and true Cape Hospitality. Do not miss the traditional afternoon tea in the lounge! This Orient Express Hotel is also a member of the Leading Hotels of the World Association.

Managing Director *Nick Seewer*
201 rooms, two heated swimming pools, two flood lit tennis, fully equipped gymnasium with personal trainers, business centre, hair salon and beauty salon.
76 Orange Street, Cape Town, P.O. Box 2608, Cape Town, 8000.
phone *021 483 1000* ***fax*** *021 483 1782*
e-mail *reservations@mountnelson.co.za* ***website*** *www.orient-expresshotels.com*

THE TABLE BAY *****

V & A WATERFRONT

Situated in the heart of the Waterfront, the hotel enjoys magnificent views of Table Mountain, the working harbour and the ocean. In 2002 the Table Bay was voted the best hotel in Africa and the Middle East and the fourth best hotel in the world. This deserved award from the Conde Nast Traveller Magazine also recognised the Atlantic Restaurant as one of the 50 best new restaurants in the world.

General Manager *Grant Ruddiman*
329 rooms, swimming pool, conference rooms. Table Bay at the V & A Waterfront, Cape Town. P.O. Box Table Bay Quay 6, V & A Waterfront, 8001.
phone *021 406 5000* ***fax*** *021 406 5686*
e-mail *tbhres@sunint.co.za* ***website*** *www.suninternational.com*

METROPOLITAN

Metropolitan Golf Course — ***Map reference:*** *16*

Length of Course: *5895 metres* — ***Holes:*** *9*

Type of Course: *Parkland* — ***Par:*** *72*

Visitors: *Saturdays reserved for members*

Club Professional: *Adrienne Thorne 021 434 9582*

Tuition: *Yes* — ***Club Shop:*** *Yes*

Practice Facilities: *Driving Range, putting and chipping greens*

Hire Facilities: *Clubs, trolleys, caddies*

Catering: *Bar, halfway house*

Location: *Cnr. Fritz Sonnenberg and Beach Roads, Mouille Point.*

General Manager: *Alan Rogut*

Postal address: *P.O.Box 50512, V&A Waterfront 8002*

Phone: *021 434 7808* — ***Fax:*** *021 434 3563*

e-mail: *met@mweb.co.za*

JEWEL IN THE CITY

The Metropolitan Golf Club was founded in 1895 and is one of South Africa's oldest golf clubs. The course has changed considerably over the last 107 years, but it is the changes that have taken place in recent years that make Metropolitan one of the places to play in this century. The introduction of a reticulation system has transformed the "Met" (as the members call it) into an excellent venue. The standards are well on the way to achieving the stated aim of the club, to become the "Jewel in the City", with a golf course manicured to perfection. The location already provides reason to play this surprising challenge in the City. Situated between Table Mountain and the sea, your golf experience will be blessed with stunning views of both. The holes are very well designed and there are a variety of tees and greens that ensure you have much more than a 9 hole experience. The club has also opened a driving range across from the road that leads to the sea front and borders the course. This is proving popular with tourists arriving from their winter golfing break. Having ironed out the cobwebs and any flaws in their swing, there can be no better way to start a South African golfing journey. The majestic backdrop of Table Mountain as you stand on the first tee makes for a memorable moment. Add to this several glimpses of the sea, and there's no doubt that you will enjoy this 9 hole course with 18 tees and several alternative greens.

THE COURSE

This is officially a 9 hole course but there are a variety of greens and tee's resulting in not only a different challenge for the second time round, but also an alternative visual experience.

7th Hole - Par 3 - 157 metres

The 7th is one of the shorter holes on this course but by no means the easiest. At 157 metres from the tiger tee's the 7th requires a precisely struck shot to carry mounds and bunkers that protect the green. Miss this green and you have to chip from a rather tricky lie. Make a par here and walk tall to the next tee.

16th Hole - Par 4 - 260 metres

A classic short par 4 and one of my personal favourites. The elevated back tee backs onto the historic Fort Wynard and affords the golfer a panoramic view of the golf course. The landing area off the tee is generous unless you decide to go for the green. With out of bounds and trees left, mounds, humps and deep bunkers right, the fairway appears very inviting from the tee. Played conservatively this hole provides a breathing space on an otherwise tough finishing stretch.

18th Hole - Par 4 - 360 metres

This a great finishing hole. It plays a good deal longer than its yardage suggests. The tee shot is particularly tough as the tee is nestled deep in an avenue of trees. You will need to find a narrow fairway that doglegs right between mounds and fairways. A large double green that also serves as the 9th hole is your target. Tricky pin positions easily deceive and many players will three-putt here. Fortunately, a very pleasant 19th hole is available. The first floor venue will allow you to savour the marvellous views of the area.

RADISSON HOTEL ★★★★★

WATERFRONT

Part of the international Rezidor SAS Hospitality group, this luxury hotel situated on the edge of the Atlantic Ocean, occupies an unrivalled Waterfront location, with its own private marina. A nautical theme pervades throughout this stylish modern venue with panoramic views all round. Tobago's international restaurant features global cuisine, while the bar and terrace on the water's edge, with their unsurpassed views, are a favourite meeting place for all.

General Manager *Marko Hytönen*
182 luxury rooms and suites, swimming pool, beauty salon and spa.
Beach Road, Granger Bay, P.O. Box 50041 Waterfront, 8002.
Phone*: 021 418 5729* ***fax*** *021 418 5717*
e-mail *capetown.info@radissonsas.co.za* ***website*** *www.radissonsas.com*

WINCHESTER MANSIONS ★★★★

SEA POINT, CAPE TOWN

This privately owned hotel in Sea Point's Platinum Mile has recently been superbly upgraded and now provides real quality in addition to the charm, views and wonderful atmosphere of this truly special place. The hotel has a famed central colonnaded courtyard where you can enjoy lunch, tea or an evening meal. This hotel, "Where guests are a pleasure and a privilege", was the winner of the "Best Luxury Hotel" at the 2001 & 2002 AA accommodation awards. Nils Heckscher is a personal friend and will ensure you have a memorable stay.

Manager *Nils Heckscher*
76 rooms, swimming pool, health spa, 221 Beach Road, Sea Point, 8001.
phone *021 434 2351* ***fax*** *021 434 0215*
e-mail *sales@winchester.co.za* ***website*** *www.winchester.co.za*

BREAKWATER LODGE

CAPE TOWN

Once a 19th Century prison, the Lodge today provides comfortable, inexpensive accommodation in a spectacular setting that looks out over the bay and up Table Mountain. Just a minute away from restaurants, pubs, theatres and shops, the Breakwater Lodge is perfectly positioned in the heart of Cape Town's Waterfront development. Neighbouring the CBD, it lies within easy reach of the main routes to the beaches, mountain walks and city hotspots.

General Manager *Peggy Klement*

285 rooms, conference facilities, secure parking. Portswood Road, Victoria and Alfred Waterfront, Cape Town. P.O. Box, 41465 Sea Point 8060

phone *021 406 1911* **fax** *021 406 1070*

e-mail *reserve@bwl.co.za* **website** *www.breakwaterlodge.co.za*

VICTORIA & ALFRED ★★★★

WATERFRONT, CAPE TOWN

Situated in the bustling Waterfront, this ideally located hotel is close to a multitude of restaurants, cinemas and shops, as well as historical places of interest. You can wander for hours exploring everything on offer or you can sit on the terrace of the Waterfront Cafe and enjoy an alfresco meal while watching the activities of a fully working dock. All of the spacious bedrooms offer a choice of superb views of the Table Bay, the majestic Table Mountain or the original Waterfront buildings.

General Manager *Andy Nold*

68 rooms, modern conference facilities. Waterfront. P.O. Box 50050, Waterfront, Cape Town, 8002.

phone *021 419 6677* **fax** *021 419 8955*

e-mail *res@vahotel.co.za* **website** *www.vahotel.co.za*

MOWBRAY

Mowbray Golf Course

Length of Course: *5770 metres*

Type of Course: *Parkland*

Holes: *18*

Par: *72*

MOWBRAY

Mowbray Golf Course
Map reference: 19
Length of Course: 5770 metres
Holes: 18
Type of Course: Parkland
Par: 72
Visitors: Booking essential
Club Professional: Greg McDonald 021 689 2811
Tuition: Yes
Club Shop: Yes
Practice Facilities: Putting greens
Hire Facilities: Clubs, trolleys, caddies and drive carts (bookings essential)
Catering: Bar, restaurant, halfway house
Location: Alexander Road, Pinelands
General Manager: David Duncan
Postal address: P.O.Box 38003, Howard Place 7450
Phone: 021 685 3018
Fax: 021 686 6008
e-mail: mowbray@global.co.za
web: www.mowbraygolfclub.co.za

RISING OF THE PHOENIX

At precisely 3.05 am on the 31st October1993, an electrical fault in the bar at Mowbray Golf Club caused a spark that started a fire. Those of us familiar with the Cape will understand that the southeaster wind gusting that night fanned the flames to such an extent that, in only forty five minutes, the Club was totally demolished.

The timing was particularly inopportune as the course had just been upgraded and was about to show its new face to both tournament players and the general public during the Bells Cup held annually in January at this venue.

However, out of all bad, comes some good. The good news is that a new R3,5 million Club house has arisen from the ashes and in the intervening years both members and visitors have enjoyed not only the rebuilt clubhouse facilities but also the excellent re-design improvements of what was already a challenging course.

The course is parkland and improvements were made to the flat greens. They have been enlarged and subtle slopes have been introduced. Water hazards have been extended and a few new ones put in. One definite advantage is the drainage ditches introduced along some fairways - that is, unless you land in them! As Mowbray was traditionally a very wet winter course, these ditches now ensure a much better year round standard.

As is the case on many of Cape Town's courses, trees stand sentry on the fairways that have been narrowed by introducing some new fairway bunkers.

THE COURSE

1st Hole - Par 4 - 269 metres

This hole doglegs right. Though it is short, it requires an accurate tee shot to avoid one left hand bunker and three bunkers set in the fairway on the right. All three bunkers are easily carried with a wood or long iron, but anything less than accurate will run out of fairway into trees on the left. The second shot is to a large, undulating green protected by two front bunkers.

2nd Hole - Par 4 - 367 metres

The tee shot should be just left of the right hand fairway bunker which can be easily carried. The fairway is lined by trees on both sides and two fairway mounds, one on the right and one further left towards the green, can create problems with distance and any shot that is too big will find a third bunker to the back. Too far right and a sharp slope will take you towards an out of bounds.

3rd Hole - Par 4 - 312 metres

The fairway has trees on both sides, but it is those on the right that will intimidate you most. Consequently, the tee shot should be to the left hand side of the fairway. A large water hazard on the right, in front of the green, will, no doubt, surprise you as it is not easily noticed from the fairway. A second shot which is too far left will catch a small bunker halfway up the left hand side of the green and a shot, carrying the water, too far right, will find two bunkers waiting.

Gould's special note:

Look out for the spectacular 15th hole with Maclear's Beacon on the flank of Table Mountain rising high above the stone pines.

THE AREA

Mowbray Golf Club is situated near the pleasant, leafy suburb of Pinelands. If you take a drive through this area, you will get a feel of the residential suburbs of Cape Town. The shopping area of Rondebosch, and the upmarket Cavendish Square in Claremont, are nearby, and so too is the State President's house, "Groote Schuur". Rhodes Memorial is worth visiting for the great view the Hottentots-Holland provides of the southern parts of Cape Town and across to the long chain of mountains that stretch from False Bay to the north for a hundred kilometres.

THE COURTYARD ★★★★

MOWBRAY, CAPE TOWN

This hotel, part of a national chain, has a prime location overlooking the Liesbeeck River wetlands and affords stunning views of Devil's Peak Mountain. The Manor House, a National Monument, has been beautifully restored and houses the reception, restaurant, lounge and small meeting room. The layout of the hotel, with several courtyards, is spacious and the bedrooms tastefully decorated. The colossal wild fig tree at the entrance is quite spectacular.

Manager *Edward Williams*

70 suites, swimming pool , 12 seater boardroom , guest office ,internet facilities.

Liesbeek Avenue, Mowbray. P.O. Box 13157, Mowbray, 7705.

phone *021 448 3929* ***fax*** *021 448 5494*

e-mail *cyct.resv@citylodge.co.za* ***website*** *www.citylodge.co.za*

CITY LODGE PINELANDS ★★★

MOWBRAY, CAPE TOWN

This hotel is part of the National City Lodge Hotel Group whose selected service hotels are specifically geared for the travelling businessman. It is also ideal for the golfer as the hotel is right on the Mowbray golf course - walk out through the pool door and you will be on the first green! The framed golf ball, surrounded by shattered glass, which hangs at the reception desk, is evidence of some golfer's poor slice!

Manager *Dean Samouilhan*

133 rooms, swimming pool, gym, 12 seater boardroom, internet facilities.

Raapenberg Road, Mowbray. P.O. Box 124, Howard Place, 7450.

phone *021 685 7944* ***fax*** *021 685 7997*

e-mail *clpine.resv@citylodge.co.za* ***website*** *www.citylodge.co.za*

RONDEBOSCH

Rondebosch Golf Course
Length of Course: *5712 metres*
Type of Course: *Parkland*
Holes: *18*
Par: *72*

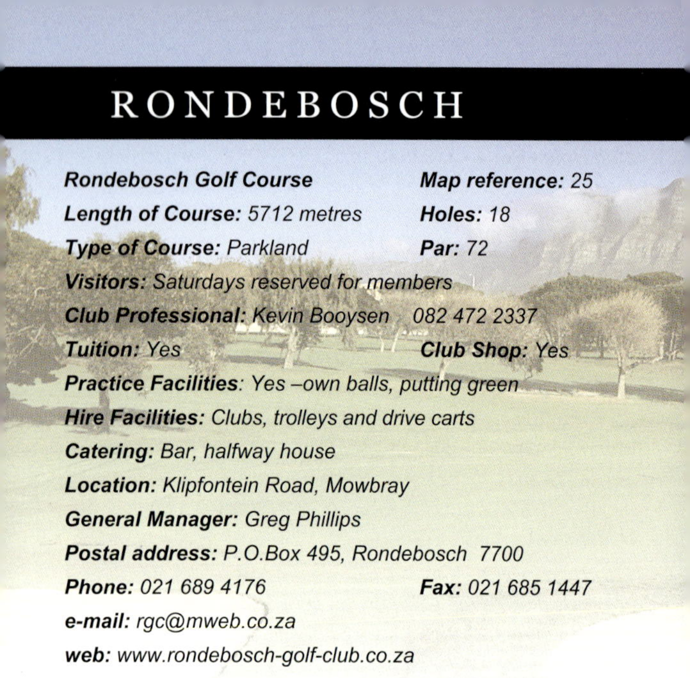

RONDEBOSCH

Rondebosch Golf Course | **Map reference:** *25*
Length of Course: *5712 metres* | **Holes:** *18*
Type of Course: *Parkland* | **Par:** *72*
Visitors: *Saturdays reserved for members*
Club Professional: *Kevin Booysen 082 472 2337*
Tuition: *Yes* | **Club Shop:** *Yes*
Practice Facilities: *Yes –own balls, putting green*
Hire Facilities: *Clubs, trolleys and drive carts*
Catering: *Bar, halfway house*
Location: *Klipfontein Road, Mowbray*
General Manager: *Greg Phillips*
Postal address: *P.O.Box 495, Rondebosch 7700*
Phone: *021 689 4176* | **Fax:** *021 685 1447*
e-mail: *rgc@mweb.co.za*
web: *www.rondebosch-golf-club.co.za*

CANAL CORNER

Rondebosch Golf Club, situated between two busy highways, has over several years, completed a successful and ambitious upgrading programme. The resulting improvements have succeeded in creating a truly well manicured year-round golf course. These improvements have been appreciated by the professional golfers who participate in the Vodacom Tournament, one of South Africa's PGA events on the local tour, held there annually.

The course is criss-crossed by canals and is fairly hilly in places. As is true of most courses in the Cape, this one has two faces. In winter, there is the northwest wind to contend with and in summer, the course grits its teeth against the notorious Southeaster. The canals necessitate some long carries over water (a word of warning - they can be wider than they look!) and you will be hitting shots to greens both below and above you. The clubhouse and pro-shop cater for all your requirements and the club has a deserved reputation as a welcoming and social venue.

Gould's special note:

The improvements at Rondebosch have included renovations to the clubhouse. I have to make special mention of the friendliness of the members. A visit to the upstairs bar will explain all!

THE COURSE

16th Hole - Par 4 - 318 metres

A recently introduced water feature that dissects the 16th and 17th holes has created both a visual as well as an added challenge to both holes. The hole is a dogleg left, curving around a canal, which hugs the left hand fairway. As you stand on the tee overlooking the canal, the twin towers of the power station lie directly ahead. The fairway is situated well to the right and your best line is to aim to the second fairway mound. (Long hitters will brave a tighter line). The second shot heads back towards the water. The green is large and undulating with two bunkers on the right. If you hit left, you'll probably be pleased to be in the front left hand bunker instead of the canal! Accuracy and correct club selection are imperative on this short par 4.

17th Hole - Par 5 - 466 metres

Water on the left and water on the right are considerations that lead to a conservative approach off the tee. A solitary pine to the left of the fairway will correctly tell you that anywhere to the right of this tree is suitable for this sharp dogleg left. Any shot to the left will land you either in the water, in trees or out of bounds. Very long hitters, however, should worry about the canal that runs alongside the right and crosses the fairway. The second shot needs to carry the canal to a narrow fairway lined on both sides by trees. The bunker-less green, nevertheless, has Scottish style swales surrounding it and it slopes steeply from front to back.

18th Hole - Par 4 - 300 metres

Out of bounds feature all the way down the left hand side of this hole and trees on the right require an accurate drive to the undulating, narrow fairway. The fairway mounds will, no doubt, give you a downhill or uphill shot to a green slightly above you. A very large right hand front bunker and a smaller version on the front left are the only protection for the green.

THE AREA

As you look back at Table Mountain from the course, you will see the distinguished, red roof buildings that make up the University of Cape Town.

Nearby is Rhodes Memorial, a monument to the brooding empire builder, Cecil John Rhodes, which is worth visiting both for a magnificent view of Cape Town and for a pleasant afternoon tea.

For the shopper you can visit the major Southern Suburbs shopping mall of Cavendish Square, situated in Claremont.

GREENWAYS ★★★★

UPPER CLAREMONT, CAPE TOWN

Greenways is a gracious homestead situated on 6 acres of magnificent landscaped gardens and enchanting woodlands. This tranquil estate has breathtaking views of Mountains and gardens and is 12 minutes from Cape Town City centre. After relaxing in the spacious, individually decorated rooms, strolling in the majestic gardens or basking beside the sparkling pool, your stay will be enhanced by the cordon-bleu cuisine and the fine service of this elegant hotel.

Manager *Karen Kitshoff*

5 suites, 1 family suite, 8 luxury rooms, swimming pool, croquet, tennis court, beauty salon, conference facilities. 1 - 5 Torquay Avenue, Upper Claremont, 7708.

phone *021 761 1792* ***fax*** *021 761 0878*

e-mail *reservations@greenways.co.za* ***website*** *www.greenways.co.za*

THE AMBASSADOR ★★★★

BANTRY BAY, CAPE TOWN

Perched high above the rocks overlooking the Cape Peninsula's famous Atlantic coastline, spectacular views are matched by the service and hospitality of this fine hotel. There is a choice of elegantly appointed rooms or fully equipped Executive Suites and the bar and Waves restaurant hug the cliffs offering uninterrupted ocean views. Close to the City, the Waterfront area and within walking distance of the famed Clifton and Camps Bay beaches.

General Manager *Martin Fowler*

69 rooms, 29 executive suites, swimming pool

34 Victoria Road, Bantry Bay, Cape Town, 8001. P.O. Box 83, Sea Point, Cape Town, 8060.

phone *021 439 6170* ***fax*** *021 439 6336*

e-mail *reservations@ambassador.co.za* ***website*** *www.ambassador.co.za*

The PENINSULA
ALL-SUITE-HOTEL

SUMMIT
HOTELS & RESORTS

Just a short distance from the Cape's famous Victoria & Alfred Waterfront, The Peninsula is the place to stay in Cape Town. The hotel's exclusive suites all enjoy stunning views over the sea and the select stretch of pristine coastline known as the 'Platinum Mile' ... and there is even a golf course nearby too.

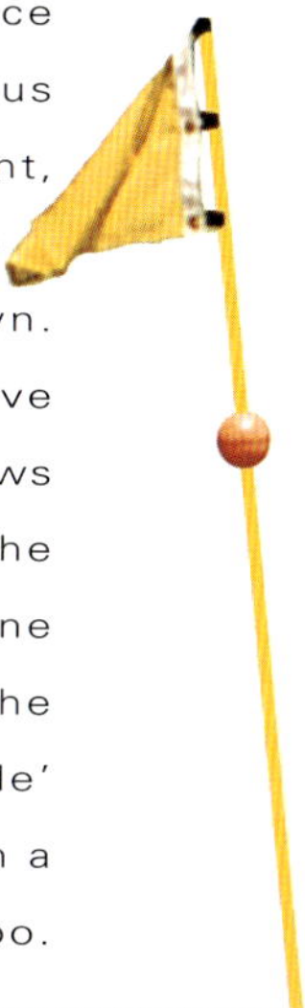

Three Cities
RICA'S EXCEPTIONAL HOSPITALITY GROUP

www.threecities.co.za

eninsula All Suite Hotel,
PO Box 768, Sea Point, 8060,
Cape Town, South Africa

website: www.peninsula.co.za
e-mail: reserve@peninsula.co.za

STEENBERG

Steenberg Golf Estate

Length of Course: *6115 metres*

STEENBERG

Steenberg Golf Course | **Map reference:** 29
Length of Course: 6115 metres | **Holes:** 18
Type of Course: Parkland | **Par:** 72
Visitors: Restricted to Members, guests and Hotel guests
Club Professional: Dave Cooke 021 713 2233
Tuition: Yes | **Club Shop:** Yes
Practice Facilities: Practise tee –club balls, putting and chipping greens
Hire Facilities: Clubs, trolleys, caddies and drive carts (bookings essential)
Catering: Bar, restaurant, halfway house
Location: Corner Tokai and Steenberg Roads, Constantia Valley
Contact: Mike Russell
Address: 1111 Steenberg Estate, Tokai Road, Tokai 7945
Phone: 021 713 2233 | **Fax:** 021 713 2231
e-mail: mrussell@zsd.co.za

GREEN HAVEN

From the first day of play, Steenberg has received a deserved reputation for its magnificent greens. This remains a fact several years later as you play this course set under beautiful mountain surrounds and meandering through the vineyards of South Africa's oldest wine farm. The location of this Real Estate, Hotel and Golf Course development, nestling under the Constantiaberg Mountains in the Constantia Valley, provides so many glorious views of vines, pines, bush and the mountain flora. This, added to the well manicured fairways and greens of the golf course, explains why the estate can easily be described as a Green Haven.

Steenberg (which means 'Mountain of Stone') has proved to be one of South Africa's most successful new golf developments. This is no doubt due to the aforementioned location, but also to the attention to detail both on and off the golf course.

All of the properties that surround the estate have been meticulously designed to blend in with the historical aspects of the working wine farm and the area. This design detail has also been incorporated in the splendid clubhouse. Here you will find spacious lounges, a stylish members-bar and a well stocked and well run pro-shop. Without doubt though, the memorable part of your visit will be the well appointed and immaculately kept changing rooms.

On the course, the introduction of plants, flowers and trees to enhance the existing visual beauty, has been fanatically monitored to ensure everything is truly indigenous.

To complement this attention to the environment, Peter Matkovich was chosen to design the Steenberg golf course.

His quoted slogan, that good golf course architects "listen to the land", proved ideal. Here he has followed the gentle natural slopes of the estate and created a challenge by introducing large waste bunkers, running creeks, water hazards and those excellent greens.

THE COURSE

Having identified the greens for special praise, I must mention that this should not detract from the quality of the fairways or the rest of the course. Large aprons around the greens are another special feature and the vineyards really do provide a unique visual aspect as well as a charming added hazard.
I have chosen the opening three holes to describe below but in passing I must mention there are wonderful par threes on this course highlighted by the green on the fourteenth hole which must qualify as the longest green I have ever played! It is 72 Metres from front to back.

1st Hole - Par 4 - 373 metres

This has a slight dogleg to the right and longer hitters will have to thread the fairway bunkers that protect either side. Playing short of these bunkers will require a good second to an elevated green protected by only one bunker. The real protection, however, are the slopes around this elevated target.

2nd Hole - Par 3 - 163 metres

The first of Steenberg's excellent short holes has three bunkers to be carried in order to hit the green. These bunkers also create a degree of difficulty regarding perspective. This is because they are well short of the green that sits in a grassy bowl. The green has a subtle two tier aspect and pin position should be checked prior to the tee shot.

3rd Hole - Par 4 - 371 metres

The Silvermine Mountain is the backdrop to a fairway narrowing between trees at the landing area off the tee. From the tee you will get a sense that the fairway runs downhill and indeed this is a fact. The fairway runs gently downwards to a green seemingly only guarded by a copse of trees on the right and a steep bank to the left. However four back bunkers are prepared to receive any shot too long.

STEENBERG HOTEL ★★★★★

CAPE TOWN

This 5-star graded Country Hotel is situated on the Cape's oldest working wine farm, a mere 20 minutes from the City Centre. The twenty-four bedroom hotel nestles in the tranquil Constantia Valley, against the slopes of the Steenberg Mountain, offering sweeping views over False Bay. The hotel buildings, dating back to 1862, encompass the elegant rooms and Catharina's Restaurant, famed for its fine fare and superb wines.

General Manager *Eddie van Zyl*

24 rooms, swimming pool, conference facilities, wine cellar.

10802 Steenberg Estate, Tokai Road, Tokai, 7945.

phone *021 713 2222* ***fax*** *021 713 2251*

e-mail *reservations@steenberghotel.com* ***website*** *www.steenberghotel.com*

HIGH TIMBERS LODGE

CAPE TOWN

Secluded in a 1.5 acre lush, landscaped garden, this luxurious owner-managed lodge provides true hospitality in a tranquil setting, blessed with panoramic views, over Table Mountain nature reserve and the Constantia Vineyards below, framed by distant mountains. From their high vantage location, each en-suite bedroom encompasses the personal touch of Oliver and Coleen, your hosts, while allowing marvellous views of the beautifully manicured gardens and the splendid natural canvas of this beautiful area. Breakfasts here are a legend!

Owners *Coleen and Oliver Jacobs*

6 rooms, swimming pool, secure parking. 126 Zwaanswyk Road, Tokai, Cape Town, 7945.

phone *021 713 2126* ***fax*** *021 713 2127*

e-mail *oliver@hightimberslodge.co.za* ***website*** *www.hightimberslodge.co.za*

WESTLAKE

Westlake Golf Course

Length of Course: *5750 metres*

WESTLAKE

Westlake Golf Course **Map reference:** 32
Length of Course: 5750 metres **Holes:** 18
Type of Course: Parkland **Par:** 72
Visitors: Saturdays reserved for members
Club Professional: Clive Holmes 021 788 2011
Tuition: Yes **Club Shop:** Yes
Practice Facilities: Chipping area, putting green, driving range
Hire Facilities: Clubs, trolleys, drive carts and caddies
Catering: Bar, restaurant, halfway house
Location: Westlake Avenue, Lakeside, 7945
Contact: GM-Mike McAloon / Club Man - Doug Bain
Phone: 021 788 2020 **Fax:** 021 788 2530
e-mail: wgc@westlakegolfclub.co.za **web:** www.westlakegolfclub.co.za

TOWERING PINES

Towering flat pines are the main feature of this course. These stately trees create natural avenues for some of the fairways, while a variety of indigenous bush and a mix of small and large trees are the other available hazards to guard the path to the greens. Westlake lies in the shade of the slopes of Silvermine Mountain near the seaside town of Muizenberg. Lush vegetation and shrubs frame the greens and the course always seems to be ablaze with colour.

Westlake has regularly undergone upgrading alterations over several years. This has involved, among other things, the introduction of a new short par three hole. The greens are in excellent condition year round and can be on the quick side when freshly cut. In recent years, several new bunkers have been added, though this has not impacted on the sense of space given by many wide fairways. However, it is wise not to become too complacent as the aforementioned trees should keep you focused on the need for accuracy.

The clubhouse, situated at the face of Silvermine Mountain, has recently had a magnificent face lift and now has all the facilities expected of a modern club. You can sit on the brick paved terrace overlooking the18th green or pop upstairs for a good-value meal in the restaurant. The bar and lounge, which are also upstairs, offer an uninterrupted view of False Bay and the distant Helderberg Mountains.

Gould's special note:

I've always enjoyed this club, not only for the course, but also for its excellent social atmosphere. Westlake enjoys a good mix of male and female members - maybe that's the secret!

THE COURSE

10th Hole - Par 4 - 376 metres

This par 4 has the tall, flat pines in the play from the tee. They stand on the right of the fairway and the tee shot must stay to the left. There is a gentle dogleg right with the fairway running downhill to a green surrounded by a high bank.

11th Hole - Par 4 - 331 metres

Trees abound here. On the left, they line the length of the fairway. In past years a large tree encroached on the fairway. These days it is no longer a penalising hazard. Nevertheless a long to mid-iron will be needed to avoid the protection at the green. There is a bunker and a severe slope to the left. Stay left off the tee and right with your second shot.

12th Hole - Par 4 - 367 metres

The elevated tee provides a good view of the fairway below as it funnels to the left. Trees to the left of the turn narrow your target in the landing area. There are more pines to the right and, just short of the green, is another of Westlake's giant pines. Your shot will need to stay just left of this tree. The green is long and fairly close to an out of bounds fence to the left.

Gould's special note:

The halfway house here sets standards for all the other clubs to aspire to.

THE AREA

Rudyard Kipling once wrote of this area, "White as the sands of Muizenberg spun before the gale." Taking a walk along Muizenberg's lengthy, broad, sandy beach is as popular with locals as it is with visitors - and this resort offers beach front activities for the kids with a giant water slide, swimming pools and a putt-putt course, as well as good surfing in warm water. At nearby St James, there is a small beach, usually sheltered from the wind, where you will find tidal pools ideal for swimming. (The multi-coloured changing booths here always remind me of my northern French background!) One of my favourite spots is the Brass Bell restaurant in Kalk Bay. It has a small, welcoming pub and the seafood is noteworthy.

WHALE COTTAGE CAMPS BAY★★★★

CAMPS BAY, CAPE TOWN

This stately home, with unique marine décor and magnificent ocean views, is situated only 500 meters from the famous Camps Bay beach, and within walking distance of over 25 restaurants. Comfortable rooms and a choice of two swimming pools, as well as secure parking, are the added features. This delightful bed and breakfast venue was selected as one of the top 10 B&B's, featured in Vogue Magazine. Wir sprechen Deutsch.

Owner *Christiane von Ulmenstein*

6 rooms, air-conditioning in seafacing rooms, 2 swimming pools, secure parking. Whale Cottage loyalty card. 57 Camps Bay Drive, Camps Bay, 8005.

phone *021 438 3840* **fax** *021 438 4388*

e-mail *campsbay@whalecottage.com* **website** *www.whalecottage.com*

WHALE COTTAGE BAKOVEN★★★★

BAKOVEN, CAPE TOWN

Whale Cottage Bakoven is one of a quartet of award winning guesthouses that have been featured in Vogue, Femina, Fairlady and other leading magazines. The other two, in Camps Bay and Hermanus, share the same facilities such as swimming pool, tea and coffee facilities, radio/alarm clock and an Internet facility. The cottage has 5 delightful en-suite rooms, each allowing breathtaking sea views of Camps Bay and Bakoven. Wir sprechen Deutsch.

Owner *Christiane von Ulmenstein*

5 rooms, swimming pool. Whale Cottage loyalty card.

50 Victoria Road, Bakoven, Camps Bay. P.O. Box 32024, Camps Bay, 8040

phone *021 438 3840* **fax** *021 438 4388*

e-mail *bakoven@whalecottage.com* **website** *www.whalecottage.com*

CAPE SUITES HOTEL ★★★★

CAPE TOWN

Nestled at the foot of Table Mountain, with views of the Cape Town city skyline and Table Bay, lies the Best Western Cape Suites Hotel - a village style hotel with 123 studio, one, two and three bedroom suites. The hotel is a 5-minute drive to the famous V&A Waterfront and 15 minutes from the beaches of Camps Bay and Clifton. Guests will enjoy a home-away-from-home environment in spacious, air-conditioned apartments equipped with kitchens filled to a four star standard.

General Manager *Nelson Rodrigues.*
123 studios, one, two and three bedroom suites, 2 swimming pools, 2 bars.
Corner of De Villiers & Constitution Streets. P.O. Box 51085, Waterfront, 8002
phone *021 461 0727* ***fax*** *021 462 4389*
e-mail *info@capesuites.co.za* ***website*** *www.capesuites.co.za*

OCEAN VIEW ★★★★

CAMPS BAY, CAPE TOWN

Ocean View House in Camps Bay/Bakoven, is a luxurious establishment with superb views of the Atlantic. The rooms and suites, including the presidential suite, are all sea facing. Each has either a balcony or garden terrace, insuring memorable views. Facilities include a swimming pool and beautifully landscaped gardens, koi pond and ample parking. Ocean View is an ideal location for visiting the city, the majestic beaches or exploring the wonders of the Cape.

General manager *Mark Goveia.*
14 rooms, swimming pool, secure parking. 33 Victoria Road, Bakoven, Camps Bay, Cape Town, 8005
phone *021 438 1982* ***fax*** *021 438 2287*
e-mail *oceanv@mweb.co.za* ***website*** *www.oceanview-house.com*

CLOVELLY

Clovelly Golf Course

Length of Course: *5908 metres*

CLOVELLY

Clovelly Golf Course | **Map reference:** 4

Length of Course: 5908 metres | **Holes:** 18

Type of Course: Parkland | **Par:** 72

Visitors: Saturdays reserved for members, bookings recommended all year

Club Professional: Dave Odendaal 021 782 6410

Tuition: Yes | **Club Shop:** Yes

Practice Facilities: Putting greens

Hire Facilities: Clubs, trolleys, caddies and drive carts

Catering: Bar, restaurant, halfway house

Location: Clovelly Road, Clovelly

Contact: Jeremy Lindquist

Phone: 021 782 1118 | **Fax:** 021 782 6853

e-mail: clubhouse@global.co.za | **web:** www.clovelly.co.za

PICK 'n PLAY

Clovelly Golf Course and Country Club is situated between the villages of Fish Hoek and Kalk Bay. It is owned by Mr Raymond Ackerman, chairman of the vast and efficient supermarket chain, Pick 'n Pay, and it is a favourite course among visiting overseas guests, not only for its lush appearance, but also for its excellent clubhouse facilities.

The course, that has enjoyed a long term reputation for its year round condition, has in recent times further enhanced its charm with the introduction of new water features. These visually pleasing features impact on the first and the seventeenth holes. However, it is at the short 11th, that the water and alterations create a superb picture to cherish. The Clubhouse, which has also enjoyed an upgrade of its already worthy facilities recently, is perched high above the course, from where you have a vantage point over not only the 18th hole, but also the 1st and 10th holes which both feature sharp doglegs, to the right and left respectively. This will immediately tell you that accurate tee shots are required, something you will be reminded of constantly on this narrow course. During the summer months, you can expect to have a little (and sometimes, a lot of) wind which adds to the difficulty on this very attractive course.

THE COURSE

7th Hole - Par 4 - 349 metres

The high tee, in the shadow of the mountain on the left, gives you a good view of this hole that doglegs to the left. You have a narrow target at which to aim and the fairway slopes from left to right. Trees on the left will have you aiming to the right where there is more space, but be careful, for trees await you if your shot is too long. The second shot is to an uphill green protected by bunkers on each side leaving a narrow entrance to negotiate.

8th Hole - Par 3 - 185 metres

This is a really challenging short hole, even in calm conditions. The green nestles below a bank to the right and has a big fall away to the left. The green is long and two-tiered and it is important to note the pin placement when selecting your club. Try to stay right, as the bank will assist your ball back to the green. A shot to the left will result in a tough shot back up to this tricky green and trees may hinder your swing.

9th Hole - Par 5 - 481 metres

To have a par 5 hole as a stroke 1 will tell you that this is a particularly punishing hole that has many moods, depending on the prevailing wind. It is a long curving hole to the left and your aim will be to the right of the fairway that narrows before moving uphill to the green. There is a steep slope to the right of the green that will ensure that your ball scampers away from the target. Out of bounds on the left will tell you that you need a precise third shot to this very tough hole.

THE AREA

Kalk Bay is a quaint fishing harbour from where the fishermen set off daily in search of Kabeljou, Yellowtail and Snoek. Close by, Fish Hoek features calm waters and a sandy beach ideal for swimming. Many regattas are held here during the year and you may be lucky enough to enjoy the sight of the multi-coloured catamaran sails dotted across the bay.

If you have time, take a drive through Fish Hoek, past Glencairn and on to Simonstown, the naval base. Simonstown has a rich and fascinating history and its age is indicated by the fact that there are no fewer than 21 buildings over 150 years old. There are many museums, monuments and statues to visit but perhaps the most well known is the statue of Able Seaman Just Nuisance, a Great Dane adopted as a mascot by the sailors in World War II. Boulders Beach, in Simonstown, is home to a penguin colony and watching them waddle about and take a dip in the sea is delightful.

ALPHEN HOTEL ★★★★

CONSTANTIA, CAPE TOWN

Where squirrels frolic under majestic oaks; where the gleaming patina of antique furniture reflects intriguing tales of a bygone era. "Alphen - where warm Cape hospitality has reigned supreme since the 18th Century." Just 15 minutes from the centre of Cape Town, or less to mos major golf courses, Alphen gives easy access to all the Peninsula has to offer. Truly spacious bedrooms and an historic Manor House continu to provide the tradition of true Cape hospitality.

Owner *Nicky Cloete*

34 Rooms, swimming pool, health and beauty salon, hair dresser and conference facilities

Alphen Drive, Constantia. P.O. Box 35, Constantia, 7848.

phone *021 794 5011* ***fax*** *021 794 5710*

e-mail *reservations@alphen.co.za* ***website*** *www.alphen.co.za*

TARRAGONA LODGE ★★★★

HOUT BAY

Six courses within a twenty minute leisurely drive, combined with panoramic scenery and friendly warmth make this venue a must for golfers seeking service excellence. Itinerary planning is a pleasure, be it for golf or leisure, and includes forward bookings, car hire and transfers Set in a beautiful valley, the lodge offers executive luxury with persona service. Hot and cold pools sparkle in this landscaped estate.

Owner and Manager *Rodney Boast*

10 suites, hot & cold pools, conference venue

cnr of Disa River Road and Valley Road, Hout Bay. P.O. Box 26887, Hout Bay, 7872.

phone *021 790 5080* ***fax*** *021 790 5095*

e-mail *lodge@tarragona.co.za* ***website*** *www.tarragona.co.za*

MOONGLOW ★★★

SIMON'S TOWN

The spectacular views over False Bay are only surpassed by the warm welcome you receive from the O'Leary family. The en suite rooms and the spacious deck all allow the opportunity to savour the panoramic vistas from a high vantage point of this scenic area. Gould's special note: Gillian and Glynn O'Leary are personal friends and partners in my business. Mention my name and beware, they may charge you double!

Owner *Gillian O'Leary*
5 rooms. 7 Bennett Close, Cairnside, Glencairn, Simon's Town.
P.O. Box 22544, fish hoek, 7974
phone *021 786 5902* ***fax*** *021 786 5902*
e-mail *seaview@moonglow.co.za* ***website*** *www.moonglow.co.za*

IMON'S TOWN QUAYSIDE HOTEL★★★★

SIMON'S TOWN

Few towns in the Western Cape can match Simon'sTown for its combination of a naturally beautiful setting plus charming historic appeal. Home to the Royal Navy from 1812 to 1957, parts of Simon'sTown are little changed over the past two centuries. Situated within Simon's Town's own Waterfront Centre, the 4-star Quayside Hotel offers magnificent views of the harbour and distant Muizenberg Mountains. Well-known attractions within a 20-minute drive include the African Penguin Colony at the Boulders, plus the world famous Cape Point at the Cape Point National park.

Manager *Jeremy Wagner*
Jubilee Square, St George's Street, Simon's Town. PO Box 555, Simon's Town 7995
phone *021 786 3838* ***fax*** *021 786 2241*
e-mail *info@quayside.co.za* ***website*** *www.quayside.co.za*

KING DAVID

King David Golf Course

Length of Course: *6065 metres*

KING DAVID

King David Golf Course **Map reference:** *12*
Length of Course: *6065 metres* **Holes:** *18*
Type of Course: *Parkland* **Par:** *72*
Visitors: *Saturdays reserved for members*
Club Professional: *Richard Pickering 021 934 3056*
Tuition: *No* **Club Shop:** *Yes*
Practice Facilities: *Yes - own balls, putting greens*
Hire Facilities: *Clubs, trolleys, caddies and drive carts*
Catering: *Bar, halfway house*
Location: *Palotti Road, Montana, Philippi*
Contact: *Haley Bourgstein, Valery Oron*
Postal address: *P.O.Box 57, Parow, 7499*
Phone: *021 934 0365* **Fax:** *021 934 4179*
e-mail: *clubpro@mweb.co.za* **web:** *www.kingdavid@iafrica.com*

ON A ROLL

For many years this club was the least known in the Cape. The club, situated near the Cape Town Airport, has however greatly increased in profile recently due to several improvements. Most noticeable is the modern and spacious clubhouse that sets a quality tone to the visit here.

Laid out forty-five years ago, this golf course has a very different character from other Cape Town courses. Rolling fairways thread their way through the blue gum trees and it is rare to see other players as you tackle your private hole. The course is well laid out and makes good use of the available natural terrain. Until recently, sandy rough and mounds made straying off the fairways a less than pleasurable experience, but a sprinkler system introduced in recent years has resulted in these areas now being well grassed. New flowerbeds have been planted and these provide wonderful splashes of colour. The greens are generally protected by few bunkers, but several plateau greens necessitate careful club selection and accuracy otherwise you will find yourself playing many a lofted shot back to your intended target.

Many Guinea Fowl roam around this course and King David is also host to the rare Francolin.

The greens are excellent in summer and though in the past winter-grass posed a problem, a spraying programme and drainage ditches should now ensure a better winter course.

THE COURSE

1st Hole - Par 5 - 481 metres

An elevated tee overlooks the straight, narrow, rolling fairway lined on both sides by blue gum trees. There is a bunker on the left which will catch the long drive. The second shot will need to carry the continuing undulations of the fairway, whereafter you reach a green sloping uphill from front to back and right to left. A bunker middle to back on the left welcomes the pulled shot.

6th Hole - Par 4 - 361 metres

The top of Table Mountain is perfectly framed by the line of trees that house this short, straight par 4. As you stand on the tee, you will aim for the middle of two grassy mounds and this is the ideal shot. Should you fade the ball, you might find it prudent to aim left as the trees on the right harbor a water hazard. There is no trouble in front of the green, though a bunker well left comes into play. The real concern is if your shot is too long. In that case a steep bank will push your ball towards the water.

14th Hole - Par 5 - 424 metres

For me this hole best illustrates the recent improvements to this course. In the past, a dogleg on the right meant that you always aimed at a narrow fairway and, if you missed the mown area, you were greeted with sandy lies. Now, however, your ball will be in lush semi-rough allowing for a good recovery shot. The fairway leading to the flat green narrows as trees both right and left leave a tight gap. A bunker is visible on the front left while the one on the right lies in the shadow of the trees

Gould's special note:

The 12th hole-par 3 is featured in one of Gary Player's books as a great short hole.

AREA

When the course was established in the Cape Flats, land was abundant. However, the explosive demands for land has led to a proliferation of low cost housing all around. So unless you are a photojournalist there is little in the area for the tourist.

However, the heart of Cape Town is a short drive down the N2 freeway. The pulsating heart of the City is undeniably The V&A Waterfront. With its old world buildings, filled with exotic restaurants, pubs, shopping malls, cinemas, live shows, museums, street entertainment-open air concerts, it is worth watching the passing parade of people in holiday mood and also the movement of ships, tugs, yachts and trawlers through the harbour.

TABLE MOUNTAIN LODGE ★★★

TAMBOERSKLOOF

Table Mountain Lodge nestles at the foot of Table Mountain and was originally built in 1885 on the Leeuwenvoet Estate. The lodge has been lovingly restored and consistently upgraded. There are 8 comfortable en-suite bedrooms, individually appointed. Scrumptious English breakfasts are served, while the heart of this delightful venue is the cosy pub, where your hosts Di and Janne Dagh, will welcome you with true hospitality.

Owners *Di and Janne Dagh*

8 rooms, swimming pool.

10A Tamboerskloof Road, corner Burnside Road, Tamboerskloof, Cape Town, 8001.

phone *021 423 0042* ***fax*** *021 423 4983*

e-mail *tml@iafrica.com* ***website*** *www.tablemountainlodge.co.za*

MILNERTON

Milnerton Golf Course

Length of Course: *5788 metres*

MILNERTON

Milnerton Golf Course ***Map reference:*** *17*
Length of Course: *5788 metres* ***Holes:*** *18*
Type of Course: *Links* ***Par:*** *72*
Visitors: *Booking essential*
Club Professional: *Stuart Howard 021 552 3108*
Tuition: *Yes* ***Club Shop:*** *Yes*
Practice Facilities: *Putting greens, chipping area*
Hire Facilities: *Clubs, trolleys, caddies and drive carts*
Catering: *Bar, halfway house*
Contact: *Carina Buisson*
Address: *Bridge Road, Milnerton 7441*
Phone: *021 552 1047* ***Fax:*** *021 551 5897*
e-mail: *milgolf@interkom.co.za* ***web:*** *www.golfersinformation.co.za*

TRUE LINKS

The Milnerton golf course, always famous for its superb location between sea and lagoon, has increased in reputation due to ongoing improvements. A real estate development necessitated some alterations to the layout and the members took the opportunity to upgrade, not only the links layout, but also to add new water features and bunkers and to introduce excellent new greens. Superb putting surfaces now welcome you, to add to the magnificent views of Table Mountain and its surrounds.

The third tee provides the first vantage point to the mountain and from here you will notice the sandy beach and dunes that run alongside the course.

In this area, nature also supplies wind and, in true links fashion, this will determine the degree of difficulty you will encounter. Should the southeaster be blowing, you will go out with the wind behind you and most of the first nine holes will be down wind. Once homeward bound, you will need to keep your head bowed so will be unable to look up and enjoy the mountain views too often! On a windless day, your only concern will be the bushy areas near the beach and some tree-lined fairways that are seemingly narrow. Playing a links course you will hopefully have, in your repertoire, the answer to playing sandy lies, a shot you will definitely need.

Gould's special note:
The course continues to undergo alterations due to the building of houses in the area.

THE COURSE

16th Hole - Par 4 - 290 metres

The lagoon that meanders to the left of the finishing holes makes a tough homeward stretch, beautiful. This hole has a narrow fairway and a majestic view of Table Mountain and Lions Head. The landing area seems narrow between grass bunkers right, a solitary tree beside them and water left. The second shot to this short par 4 will be a lofted iron to a wide figure eight green. Three bunkers on the right will need to be negotiated if the pin is on the right of this green.

17th Hole - Par 5 - 423 metres

The tee shot is to a truly wide landing area. The only concern will be the water to the left that accompanies the fairway to the green, but only the wildest of hooks will bring this into play. A downhill and undulating fairway flattens out at the green and the approach to the seemingly small green will need only to avoid sloping grassy banks. The target is actually larger than seen from the fairway.

18th Hole - Par 4 - 341 metres

While this hole is not seemingly long on the scorecard, it is quite a challenge if you are playing into the prevailing wind. Memorable visuals from this tee are water left and the lighthouse behind the green. Most average golfers will be hitting a long iron or wood to this final hole and the large uphill green that sits perilously close to the water will require only the best of shots to be found in two.

THE AREA

Bloubergstrand, the extensive beach nearby, is the spot from which most published photographs of Table Mountain and Table Bay are taken, which will give you an idea of the incredible views to be enjoyed from this beach. If you feel like stretching your legs, and don't mind a bit of wind, it is a great place for a long walk.

The lagoon area in Milnerton is a bird sanctuary and a popular venue for windsurfing and canoeing. A flea market is usually held on the lawns next to the lagoon on Sundays in summer and you could spend a fun couple of hours here in the sunshine.

There are many good restaurants in this area, but two worth particular mention are Maestros on the Beach (in the Lagoon area) and On the Rocks (in Bloubergstrand).

DOLPHIN BEACH HOTEL ★★★★

BLOUBERG BEACH

The hotel enjoys a unique position with direct access to the beach and unparalleled views of Table Bay and Table Mountain. There are 32 luxury apartments and rooms with a self-catering option. Its proximity to the Milnerton Golf Course and the Atlantic Beach Golf Estate makes it an ideal base for the golfer. At sunset, watch the spectacular change of colours over the sea.

***General Manager** Stuart Twine*
32 rooms, swimming pool.
Marine Drive, Blouberg.
P.O. Box 11313, Bloubergrant, 7443.
***phone** 021 557 8140* ***fax** 021 557 8147*
***e-mail** dolphinbeach@icon.co.za* ***website** www.visitdolphinbeach.com*

COTSWOLD HOUSE

MILNERTON

For over 12 years, Don and Denise Jeffery have offered warm and friendly hospitality in the gracious and relaxed surroundings of Cotswold House. Their delightful former Governor-General's Cape Dutch home, offers charming en-suite bedrooms and a huge sparkling swimming pool. Ideally situated opposite Milnerton golf course, you are only 10 minutes away from the city centre and the Waterfront delights.

***Owners** Don and Denise Jeffery*
6 rooms, parking, swimming pool.
Cotswold Drive, Milnerton. P.O. Box 412, Milnerton, 7435.
***phone** 021 551 3637* ***fax** 021 552 4228*
***e-mail** cotswold@mweb.co.za* ***website** www.cotswoldguesthouse.com*

GOLF EQUIPMENT
IS OUR BUSINESS

- THE BEST QUALITY
- THE BEST SERVICE
- THE BEST PRICES

The GOLFERS CLUB

Bell's Golf Academy
Tyger Valley

948-5697

Take N1 North towards Paarl and exit Durbanville / Belville off ramp. Turn left and first left again at Town Lodge (on corner.) Turn left at T-junction into Carl Cronje Drive and see us 500m on right hand side.

@ PRO RANGE GOLF CENTRES

- Official handicap & affiliation through our host golf clubs
- Individual lessons.
- Junior and ladies clinics.
- Join any range and automatically become a national member.
- National membership from just R45 per month.

BELL'S Golf Academy

ATLANTIC BEACH

Atlantic Beach Golf Estate
Length of Course: *5855 metres*
Type of Course: *Links*

ATLANTIC BEACH

Atlantic Beach Golf Course — ***Map reference:*** *2*

Length of Course: *5855 metres* — ***Holes:*** *18*

Type of Course: *Links* — ***Par:*** *70*

Visitors: *Saturdays and Sunday mornings - members only*

Director of golf: *Teddy Webber*

Tuition: *Yes* — ***Club Shop:*** *Yes*

Practice Facilities*: Driving range*

Hire Facilities: *Clubs, trolleys and drive carts. No caddies*

Catering: *Bar, restaurant, halfway house*

Location: *Off the R 27- Towards Melkbosstrand*

Contact: *Cindy Sinclair*

Postal address: *Unit 1 Birkenhead, Atlantic Beach Golf Estate, Melkbosstrand 7441*

Phone: *021 553 2223* — ***Fax:*** *Fax: 021 553 2224*

e-mail: *enquiries@atlanticbeach.co.za* ***web:*** *www.atlanticbeachgolfclub.co.z*

NATURE RESERVED

The Atlantic Beach Golf Estate, on the West Coast of Cape Town, lies at the heart of a wonderful nature reserve that borders the Atlantic Ocean. Unparalleled views of Table Mountain, the ocean and endless white beaches are the punctuation points of this golfing challenge among the fynbos of a protected nature reserve.

The developers of the golf course have meticulously cared for the sensitivity of this environment. It is a feature on this course that balls landing in well-demarcated areas off the fairways are not to be retrieved as they have landed in the protected areas. This is a minor hazard, as the holes provide ample avenues for the golfer to cherish among the natural beauty of a golf course that encapsulates 'the links feel' of a layout so close to the sea.

It is indeed a golf course blessed with natural contours that sweep upwards and downwards among the dune-lined valleys. The course is set out in two nine hole loops that each return to the clubhouse. An important feature of the design is that few of the holes run in the same direction. This importance becomes apparent when the strong breezes of this area are in attendance. The variety of direction allows the golfer regular respite from the challenges of wind.

THE COURSE

There is a mixture of bunker designs on the course. Apart from the conventional sand traps, sandy wastes with fynbos integrated in them are a feature. There are no water hazards or trees but the natural fynbos of the landscape is ample enough to augment the challenge. The greens are large, sometimes huge, and many of them have big slopes that require great concentration.

Teddy Webber, the Director of Golf, described his favoured holes here.

5th Hole - Cableway

This hole has one of the best views on the course of Table Mountain and Robben Island. It is called the Cableway because it faces the mountain. This hole has a two-tier green from right to left and due to the wind, at 142 metres, can be any club from a 3 wood to a pitching wedge. Club selection is very important, as the green is 20 metres deep at its widest and 15 metres at the narrowest.

11th Hole - To the beach

As named, the hole faces the ocean. An elevated tee, with a rolling fairway over a shell waste area. A very difficult tee shot as the wind is always left to right, or right to left. A tough second shot to a slightly raised two-tier green. Club selection again is very important.

12th Hole - Island (Atlantic Beach feature hole)

As named, when you stand on this tee, it looks like the green is an island with no area to bail out. Once again a fantastic view of Table Mountain and Robben Island. This is the longest green on the course at 55 metres. Club selection, and noting the wind direction, will be of paramount importance.

THE ESTATE

The golf course is part of a highly sought after real estate development. This is understandable as living in a nature reserve, blessed with spectacular views of Table Mountain, beach and sea as well as gentle hillsides as a backdrop, is certainly a rare luxury - all within easy reach of the City. The success of this development is reflected in the sales of plots since its inception only three years ago. Alan Usher from Golf Resorts, who has been responsible for sales since the development began, says, "The success of this development is primarily due to its location. This is reflected in the fact that over 90% of sales are to Capetonians."

The architectural theme has followed the West Coast Farmhouse style of the area and the use of raw natural materials has resulted in the properties blending harmoniously into the landscape. The success of this coastal estate is complemented by the quality of facilities inside its secure gates. Tennis courts, swimming pools and a gymnasium are part of a central leisure area. The superbly appointed clubhouse offers fine dining facilities, bars, halfway house and conference facilities. This club is highly professionally run under the guidance of American import Bill Taylor and, in the pro-shop, under the guidance of well-known Director of Golf, Teddy Webber.

BLOUBERG MANOR BOUTIQUE HOTE

BLOUBERG

Blouberg Manor is situated at one of the most beautiful beaches in the world. It boasts magnificent views of Table Mountain and Robben Islanc and is a mere 40 metres from Big Bay, the main swimming beach and surf club in Bloubergstrand. The majestic Cape Dutch Manor House offers 12 memorable luxurious en-suite bedrooms, each decorated to a specific theme, offering information about a different cultural experience in the Cape.

General Manager *Una van Rhyn*
12 rooms, swimming pool, conference facilities
6 Verkoutern Street, Bloubergstrand 7441
phone *021 554 3135* ***fax*** *021 554 4918*
e-mail *bloubergmnr@mweb.co.za* ***website*** *Under construction.*

THE LODGE
at ATLANTIC BEACH

Grand Opening Spring 2003

Enjoy Grand Opening & Group Rates

"COMMITMENT TOWARDS EXCELLENCE"

THE LODGE
at ATLANTIC BEACH

"A spectacular coastal paradise located on the wonderful Atlantic Beach Golf Estate, The Lodge at Atlantic Beach offers natural golf course and nature reserve vistas all in a safe and convenient environment. Golfers can enjoy the beautiful 18 hole championship golf course while non golfers can enjoy nature walks, local beaches, dining and the many amenities located at Atlantic Beach."

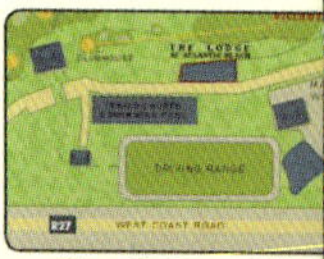

Proudly Managed by Club Innovations

ENQUIRIES
Tel/Fax: +27 21 553 4653
+27 21 553 GOLF
Email: thelodge@atlanticbeach.co.za
www.thelodgeatatlanticbeach.co.za

THE LODGE at ATLANTIC BEACH

Unit 20
Atlantic Beach Golf Esta
Birkenhead Driv
Melkbosstrand 744
Republic of South Afric

THE
GOLF
RESORTS
CLUB

LANGEBAAN

Langebaan Golf Course

Length of Course: *5823 metres*

LANGEBAAN

Langebaan Golf Course **Map reference:** 15
Length of Course: 5823 metres **Holes:** 18
Type of Course: Links **Par:** 72
Visitors: Always welcome - bookings recommended
Club Professional: None
Tuition: None **Club Shop:** Yes
Practice Facilities: Putting and chipping green
Hire Facilities: Caddies, trolleys and drive carts
Catering: Bar and halfway house
Location: Club Drive, Langebaan
Contact: Ludwig Vercuiel
Postal address: P O Box 144, Langebaan 7357
Phone: 022 772-2112 **Fax:** 022 772-2460
e-mail: lbngolf@mweb.co.za

FLAMINGOS

On my first visit to the Langebaan golf course, the brilliant blue of the dam fronting the clubhouse and the sea in the distance immediately made an impression. This alluring shade of turquoise-blue reminded me of my days in the Seychelles and the West Indies and I wish you sunny weather on your visit so that you too can experience the same feeling. As you begin to play this course, which threads its way through Karoo bush style scrubland, you will soon realize that you are certainly not in one of the above-mentioned exotic locations! The course is relatively unprotected. Low trees and bush are the only guardians and on a windy day, you will need to know how to play the low shot.

Langebaan golf course has been at the heart of real estate development, on and around the course, and the club has enjoyed a country atmosphere for many years. Excitingly, there are plans to upgrade the golf course considerably in conjunction with a new impetus of the housing projects around it.

This new impetus comes from the same developers of the real estate and upgrade of Mossel Bay in the Garden Route. A similar scenario to that of Mossel Bay will see the improvement of the shaping of fairways, the introduction of superb greens and an upgrade of the clubhouse and general facilities. This scenic spot on the West Coast of the Cape has always been cherished by Capetonians for its superb fishing, boating, beach and nature locations. Now add a championship golf course layout and I predict it will soon be discovered by the international visitor who will either decide to stay for a while, or invest in a more permanent option in this unspoilt part of the Cape.

That it's unspoilt is evident in that you will have the opportunity of seeing wild life on the course. On one particular visit, my partner and I hired two young caddies who were accompanied by their little sister. She took great delight, as we progressed around the course, in showing us the snake-eater bird and the buck that roamed the course. At one point she called me over and said "There's Flamingo's". I followed her pointing with my eyes, but there was not a flamingo in sight. She pulled me down so that I was on my haunches next to her and pointed once again. Flamingos, it turned out, was a building in the distance and the popular local dance hall!

THE COURSE

At present, many of the holes on this course look similar. I have chosen to describe one of the first nine and one of the second nine.

5th Hole - Par 3 - 158 metres

One gets a good idea of the future expansion and the development to expect of this country club when one notices the holiday homes already built to the left of this hole. A water hazard also runs along the left hand side. The green has two well shaped bunkers poised on either side of it. You will experience difficulty here if you are too long.

12th Hole - Par 5 - 464 metres

This dogleg par 5 winds its way uphill through the type of scrub typical of this course. Long hitters will cut the corner, leaving a long shot to the green above them. If the pin is right, a front bunker has to be carried and a back bunker avoided. A bunker left will trap the pulled shot. As you walk up the fairway, please stop for a second and look at the brilliant blue sea to your left.

THE AREA

Langebaan, being only an hour away from Cape Town, is an extremely popular holiday getaway spot for Capetonians. The main attraction is the 17-kilometer lagoon, which runs into the Atlantic Ocean. The lagoon is relatively sheltered and is ideal for sailing, fishing and water-skiing and it is a good spot for swimming on a hot day. If you are paddling in the shallow waters do not be surprised if you feel the earth literally moving under your feet! Harmless sand sharks love to bask in the warm sands close to the shore. The West Coast National Park nearby boasts 198 bird species and it is a delight for both bird lovers and hikers.

Many people drive to this area annually to see the famous spring flowers, which appear after the first spring rains and disappear between mid-September and October. If you're lucky enough to visit Langebaan during this time, you will be able to see carpets of these magnificent flowers providing riotous colour for miles around.

FARMHOUSE HOTEL ★★★★

LANGEBAAN

A gracious, warm and welcoming country hotel set on the hillside overlooking the tranquil Langebaan Lagoon. The original house dating back to the 1860's, has been restored in the true Cape Dutch tradition. The Restaurant, with its high ceilings and Oregon furniture, serves top class cuisine, and boasts a Diamond award-winning wine list. The gues suites, some with their own fireplaces and sweeping views of the splendi lagoon, lead to a private poolside garden.

General Manager *Dolores Eriksen*
18 rooms, swimming pool, conference facilities
5 Egret Street, Langebaan. P.O. Box 160, Langebaan.
phone *022 772 2062* **fax** *022 772 1980*
e-mail *farmhous@mweb.co.za* **website** *www.thefarmhouselangebaan.co.za*

PAROW

Parow Golf Course
Map reference: 22
Length of Course: 5976 metres
Holes: 18
Type of Course: Parkland
Par: 72
Visitors: Booking essential
Club Professional: Johan Engelbrecht 021 930 1055
Tuition: Yes
Club Shop: Yes
Practice Facilities: Putting green and chipping area
Hire Facilities: Clubs, trolleys, caddies and drive carts
Catering Facilities: Bar, halfway house
Contact: Jack Boddington
Address: Frans Conradie Drive, Parow 7500
Phone: 021 930 2160
Fax: 021 939 7756
e-mail: info@parowgolfclub.co.za
web: www.parowgolfclub.co.za

KIEWIET ATTACK

Only 20 kilometres from Cape Town, this is a busy course. With its modern clubhouse, ample parking and proximity to the N1 City shopping centre, it proves an ideal "shop and golf" venue for many a local visitor.

As you play this flat parkland style course you will note the Kiewiets. Beware! These birds nesting throughout the landscape are likely to attack you if you approach their nests too closely. There have been many new improvements to this very popular golf course. Several new bunkers, a new dam and a waste bunker are some of the new features. Also noticeable is the attention to the surrounds of the spacious clubhouse, where manicured gardens provide for a very welcoming first impression.

The three finishing holes of the first nine, listed below, will always prove to be a challenge.

The prevailing wind in the Cape is the southeaster and this makes the 9th hole, in particular, a monster. The northwester is the rain wind and, under these conditions, the 8th hole will have bogey written on your card before you even attempt the tee shot!

THE COURSE

7th Hole - Par 3 - 165 metres

A large, new elevated tee gives a view of the high bank behind the green that allows you to be bold at this long par 3, a feeling you will need, as anything hit short will land you in water! Your shot is carry all the way to the green where there is a deep bunker to the front right.

8th Hole - Par 4 - 395 metres

On this tee it is immediately obvious that the hole curves gently to the right in between an avenue of newly planted trees. This makes for a tight driving hole. There is also a drainage ditch running the length of the fairway on the right. The green sits on a slight plateau and your ball may run away from the left, that is, if you do not land in the large sand trap on that side. Two bunkers wait for any shot pushed right of the elevated, and sharply sloping green.

9th Hole - Par 4 - 392 metres

This dogleg left has a dam lining the left hand side of the fairway but this is only of concern to the big hooker as it is some distance from the mown area. The second shot will have to carry a water hazard that crosses the fairway and here, you should aim left of the grassy, tree-lined mound. The large, seemingly flat, green (there is a small slope from right to left) is surrounded by bunkers. A large boomerang shaped sand trap on the left and two more traditional ones on the right.

THE AREA

Many a long distance road traveller knows Parow, if not by name, then by the totally memorable panoramic view from the highway. For here the N1, elevated as it curves past the Tygerberg Hills, suddenly presents a big view of Table Mountain, the shining sea and setting sun almost as a reward saying "welcome home to mother!"

This is the area once designated as the site for Cape Town's 2004 Olympic bid where open spaces were rapidly being devoured for housing developments and light industrial activity. Despite not succeeding with the bid, the area continues to grow. Serving the area is the N1 City shopping complex where you will find cinemas, restaurants and a wide variety of shops. Nearby are the Grandwest Casino Complex and the Century City development that includes the Ratanga Junction theme park and Canal Walk that provides endless avenues of shops.

DURBANVILLE

Durbanville Golf Course — ***Map reference:*** *6*
Length of Course: *5916 metres* — ***Holes:*** *18*
Type of Course: *Parkland* — ***Par:*** *72*
Visitors: *Book for Wednesday and Saturday*
Club Professional: *Chris Wilkins 083 757 0447*
Tuition: *Yes* — ***Club Shop:*** *Yes*
Practice Facilities: *Putting green, practice range*
Hire Facilities: *Clubs, trolleys, caddies and drive carts*
Catering: *Bar, halfway house*
Location: *Sports Road, Durbanville*
Contact: *Fred Rees*
Postal address: *P O Box 115, Durbanville 7550*
Phone: *021 976 8121* — ***Fax:*** *021 976 0191*
e-mail: *dgmanager@durbanvillegolf.co.za*
web: *www.durbanvillegolf.co.za*

OPEN SPACES

This course, situated in Cape Town's northern suburbs, has in recent times shown considerable improvement. A long-term improvement plan by the vibrant committee is now showing results to what is becoming a fine golf venue.
The course has always enjoyed a reputation of being less demanding than the other Cape courses. Open spaces and a flat terrain allow a degree of error that will not be penalised too severely. The golf course nowadays has excellent fairways and good putting surfaces, while manicuring and the introduction of newly shaped greens have served to enhance its reputation.
The clubhouse and surrounds have had a facelift and a campaign to welcome visiting golfers will, I'm sure, achieve its goals, as you will receive a warm, friendly welcome.
Please be assured that there are some testing shots required despite the space - especially over the dam in the middle of the course.

THE COURSE

12th Hole - Par 3 - 162 metres

This hole requires a long, challenging tee shot partially over a dam. At 162 metres, the carry is also uphill to a flat green guarded only by a left hand bunker. Anything to the right will find a gentle slope edging the ball back towards the dam. The short hitter should aim for the flat fairway, visible from the tee. This shot is well left of the flag and will avoid the "splash".

13th Hole - Par 4 - 298 metres

With the dam behind you, this elevated tee offers a splendid view of the clubhouse and the Stellenbosch Mountains to your right. This short, tree-lined par 4 is probably the narrowest hole on this course. A straight drive will require a mid to short iron for the green and this shot will carry several fairway undulations. Take note of the embankment on the right otherwise your ball will be pushed away from the green into the sandy rough.

14th Hole - Par 4 - 337 metres

A wide fairway will give you time to relax before you play the second shot to a formidable green situated, it seems, in the heavens above you! Club selection is all-important here for, if you are too short, you will be playing from the bottom of the extremely steep embankment holding the large, circular green.

THE AREA

It may surprise you to know that this residential area has its own wine route! You can visit the Altydgedacht Estate where you can taste local wines or enjoy a picnic lunch. From here you may take an ox-wagon ride to another nearby estate and there is little doubt that you will enjoy the return journey in a somewhat lighter mood! Wines such as Bloemendal, Diemensdal and Neerensdal are all found in the Durbanville area.

If you enjoy the sight of thoroughbred horses thundering into action, there are polo, show jumping and regular race meetings at the Durbanville Race Course.

There is an interesting artesian well in the town where pumpkins once flourished, giving rise to the name of Durbanville's main golf tournament, "The Pampoenkraal Classic" (the Afrikaans name for pumpkin).

Bellville Golf Course **Map reference:** 3
Length of Course: 5838 metres **Holes:** 18
Type of Course: Parkland **Par:** 72
Visitors: Book for Saturdays and Wednesdays
Club Professional: Athol Day 021 913 3100
Tuition: Yes **Club Shop:** Yes
Practice Facilities: Putting and chipping greens
Hire Facilities: Clubs, trolleys, caddies and drive carts
Catering: Bar, halfway house
Contact: Gerald Smith
Postal address: P.O.Box 6186, Welgemoed 7538
Phone: 021 913 3100 **Fax:** 021 913 5121
e-mail: belgolf@isales.co.za
web: www.globaltradecentre.com/bellvillegolf

YEAR ROUND IMPROVEMENT

The Bellville Golf Club is situated in the heart of Cape Town's northern suburbs, with Bellville being a residential area overlooking the various sprawling areas making up Cape Town. The Golf Club sits in a valley and you will find yourself tackling some considerable slopes during your round.

There are two compensating factors for climbing some of these slopes - the magnificent views from the high vantage points and the standards of the shapely greens that provide a memorable putting experience throughout the course.

Indeed, the standards have consistently improved over the whole of the course, reflecting a commitment from the club members to provide a quality golfing experience to both the local and overseas visitors.

Historically, this course was very wet in winter, but in recent years a programme to provide storm water drains has resulted in a really much improved venue both in winter and summer.

The improvements are not only reflected in the drainage, but also in the attention to detail throughout the course. From the opening short and narrow par four with a blind tee shot you will enjoy a real quality round of golf.

THE COURSE

11th Hole - Par 4 - 326 metres

The locals have aptly named this hole, with its uphill dogleg to the right, 'Thrombosis'. To add to the degree of difficulty, trees on the right prevent one taking a short cut. A long second shot, uphill all the way, will have to favour the left. Anything too straight will catch a small bunker and anything too far right will encounter a steep bank precipitating the ball to a water hazard. As is generally the case at Bellville, the reward after the climb is the superb large green that allows for a variety of pin placements.

12th Hole - Par 3 - 149 metres

Catch your breath and enjoy the view over the dam before playing this tricky par 3. The tee, situated on the dam wall, sits between willow trees and the reeds fronting it. Your shot is to a green left of the dam, with any slice, push or fade guaranteed to result in your ball finding a watery grave. Too short a shot will see a steep bank rolling your ball back to the water. A large flat bunker to the left of the green may catch the less than sure, but safe, shot. Pine trees of varying sizes provide a picturesque backdrop.

13th Hole - Par 4 - 373 metres

The elevated tee gives you a pleasant view of the spacious homes surrounding the course. Your downward focus will be to a narrow fairway, protected by trees on the right and left. The prudent shot is to the left of this fairway. However, beware of a sneaky water hazard over the tree, well left of the fairway. Two bunkers guard the green and the gap between them is narrow. The left hand bunker gives a false perspective, as it is actually some way from the green. The ideal second shot is over this bunker, as even a slightly pulled shot will find a friendly slope helping the ball back towards the green. On the right you will encounter a steep downhill bank.

CLARA ANNA FONTEIN

DURBANVILLE

Only 20 minutes drive from the Waterfront is the Renosterveld tented camp at Clara Anna Fontein. The only luxury tented camp in the Wester Cape is situated in a private game reserve offering a true African bush experience, with private game drives. The 12 luxury tents all have en-suite bathrooms and are serviced daily. Eleven indigenous species of wild animals roam free on one of the last remaining indigenous bush-lands in the area.

***Owners** Justin and Tama Basson*
5 rooms, 12 luxury tents, swimming pool, conference facilities.
Visserhok Road, Durbanville. P.O. Box 1434, Durbanville 7550.
***phone** 021 975 7017* ***fax** 021 975 1533*
***e-mail** caflodge@iafrica.com* ***website** www.capetourism.org/member/claraannafontei*

CAPE
COUNTRY
ROUTES

Character, Charm & Romance

A selection of privately owned and managed hotels, guest houses and lodges along scenic and historic routes.

• 'Route 62 & Breede River Valley •
• Cedarberg & Westcoast • Garden Route & Karoo •
• Wine Routes • Whale Coast & White Sharks •
• Game & Wilderness Experience •
• Harley-Davidson Tours & Rentals •

Rufaro
DESTINATION MANAGEMENT

- Wine Tours - Local & International
- Scheduled & Tailormade Tours for Groups & Individuals
- Conference & Events

The Cape in your Glass

Room 5.3, 5th Floor, West Wing 'The Palms' Centre
145 Sir Lowry Road, Cape Town, South Africa
Tel: +27 (0) 21 462 7022/3 Fax +27 (0) 21 462 7026
Website: www.rufaro.com E-mail: rufaro@galileosa.co.za

KUILSRIVER

Kuilsriver Golf Course — ***Map reference:*** *14*

Length of Course: *5804 metres* — ***Holes:*** *18*

Type of Course: *Links/parkland* — ***Par:*** *72*

Visitors: *Always welcome - bookings recommended*

Club Professional: *Thys Potgieter 021 903 0300*

Tuition: *Yes* — ***Club Shop:*** *Yes*

Practice Facilities: *Putting and chipping green*

Hire Facilities: *Trolleys, caddies and drive carts*

Catering: *Bar, halfway house*

Location: *Bottelary Road - Cape Town to Stellenbosch*

Contact: *Joos van Zyl*

Postal address: *P.O.Box 177 Kuilsriver 7579*

Phone: *021 903 0222* — ***Fax:*** *Fax: 021 906 2197*

e-mail: *kuilgolf@mweb.co.za* — ***web:*** ***www.***sagolfinfo.com*

THE PRESSURE

The Kuilsriver golf club is the newest member club in the Cape. It was opened in 1989 and the club has blossomed in the intervening years through the dedication and passion of its founder members and subsequent committees. The course is set on the outskirts of Cape Town and borders the scenic winelands. The layout straddles an undulating landscape that is surrounded by gentle and scenic hillsides. You will inevitably note the electric Pylons that are part and parcel of the background here; however they will soon be forgotten as you will thoroughly enjoy the pressure of this tight and challenging round on a course made more interesting by excellent water features. Several of the holes are tree-lined and narrow in perspective. However, the rough here is forgiving and, when staying off the mown areas, recovery is more than possible. The clubhouse sits high above the course and the welcome here is tangible as this is a social club where visitors are encouraged, indeed cherished. The club continues to grow apace and it is a highly popular venue in the Cape winter months as it has proved to be in one of the drier areas of this scenic part of the Cape.

THE COURSE

7th Hole - Par 3 - 180 metres

This is a challenging par 3 with water fronting the tee. The water does not come in to play except as a pleasant visual. The requirements here are length and accuracy. Two bunkers have to be threaded in order to reach the large round green.

14th Hole - Par 5 - 422 metres

The surrounding hillsides are a visual delight to this short par 5. Water fronting the tee adds charm, but will not interfere in reaching a wide landing area that is narrowed by trees as the fairway curves gently right and slopes downhill to the green. The green is protected by a bunker and downhill grassy banks left and back.

17th Hole - Par 3 - 140 metres

This is a visually striking hole. The green is well below a high tee and, though there is water that has to be carried, it should not intimidate anyone except the less than confident player. A large single bunker right and a wide avenue of trees complete the picture.

Gould's special note:

A recent visiting ladies golf tour from the United Kingdom enjoyed this course immensely. They returned to play, what they considered a truly lady friendly golf course, several times.

BOSCHENMEER

Boschenmeer Golf Estate
(Paarl Golf Course)
Type of Course: *parkland*
Holes: *27*

BOSCHENMEER

Paarl Boschenmeer Golf Estate **Map reference:** 21
Length of Course: Under revision **Holes:** 27
Type of Course: Parkland **Par:** Under revision
Visitors: Booking essential
Club Professional: Ben Fouchee 082 990 7161
Tuition: Yes **Club Shop:** Yes
Practice Facilities: Yes-own balls, putting green
Hire Facilities: Clubs, trolleys, caddies and drive carts
Catering: Bar, halfway house
Location: Wemmershoek road, Paarl
Contact: Leon Scheepers
Postal address: P.O.Box 305, Paarl 7620
Phone: 021 863 1140 **Fax:** 021 863 3660
e-mail: paarlgc@mweb.co.za

A PEARL AMONG THE VINES

The sensational Paarl Valley area provides the setting for this unique 27-hole layout now at the heart of a highly successful real estate development. The original 18 holes at Paarl were always regarded as truly charming. Nestling below the famed Paarl Rock and blessed with an abundance of trees and vineyard surrounds, the course gained a reputation for its year round quality and consistency.

In recent years, the ever increasing demand for 'fairway living' in South Africa allowed for an innovative re-planning and renovation programme to the Paarl golf club.

In the latter part of 1999, nine new holes, known as the 'Boschenmeer-Nine', were introduced to accommodate the introduction of home sites, and to allow the existing 18 holes to be renovated and, indeed, improved on. The improvements are quite exceptional. David Frost, South Africa's internationally famous golfer, was retained to consult on the design of the new nine holes and the re-design of the original 18 holes. This he did, in conjunction with Danie Obermeyer of Danie Obermeyer Golf Design, who was originally involved with Fancourt in George and who gained a reputation in the Far East, before returning to South Africa to put his footprint back on his home soil. Frost is originally from the Paarl area and it is no co-incidence that he put his passion and expertise to full use in re-creating a golf course he spent many of his younger days playing on. The resulting 27 holes offer a splendid mix of tree-

lined fairways and challenging and visually spectacular water features, all leading to superb, large greens. These greens are a challenge in their own right! The 'charm' of the original Ken Elkin design has not been lost in anyway as the Berg River that runs on the southern border of the estate and the Du Toit's Kloof mountains remain wonderful natural features that serve to enhance the 27-hole challenge with scenic backdrops. Improvements continue on and around the course; at the time of writing, the superb upgrade to the original second nine holes is in play, while the first nine will be completed in 2003. The clubhouse is due to be completely redesigned and re-furbished and will include a hotel component. This will no doubt improve the facilities on offer. What cannot be improved upon, is the friendly welcome always received at this club that has a reputation for its socially active members.

Every year, this club hosts the Winelands Classic, one of the top amateur events in the country. Sponsorship and efficient organisation have turned this tournament into a splendid occasion that puts this course and the area on the tourist map.

17th hole

THE COURSE

T,he original 18 holes at Paarl are set among avenues of trees and bordered by the Berg River. The 'Boschenmeer-Nine'are more open and follow undulating terrain that traverses several powerfully visual water features.

While the upgrade of the first nine holes of the original Paarl course will be completed in 2003, the completed second nine are in play as I write and they have received acclaim from far

20th green and 21st ho

and wide, for providing the standards required by today's golfers, while maintaining the aura of a classic and traditional country course. The completed 27 holes will, I predict, result in this course becoming one of the Cape's most sought after venues.

10th Hole - Par 5 - 461 metres

This hole provides a wonderful and classic start to the second nine. There is only a narrow landing area from the tee. This is between trees on the right and a picturesque water hazard to the left. The fairway curves gently around the water and straightens to lead uphill to a large, challenging green. Bunkers short of this target make the perspective difficult.

19th Hole - Par 4 - 359 metres

This hole will focus the attention for the challenge to come. A huge dam that divides the 19th and 27th holes looms large on the left. Three bunkers wait on the right for the too cautious tee shot. The fairway sweeps gently left and water will have to be carried if the tee shot has taken a tight line to the dam. A bunker right protects a large, wide green.

27th Hole - Par 5 - 429 metres

This is a superb high-risk high-reward finishing hole. From an elevated tee the picture below is of a fairway sweeping sharply left around the spectacular dam that needs to be crossed if the player is looking for high-reward. Regular fairway bunkers on the right are to be avoided by the more prudent shots. If the pin is on the left of the green, water has to be crossed with real precision as here the green is very narrow. High, grassy banks behind will save the too long shot, but the chip back to the green is towards water! The majestic Paarl Rock adds a wonderful backdrop to a truly memorable hole.

Gould's special note:

The 22nd Hole is a majestic Par 5 hole and will be forever remembered on first playing.

THE ESTATE: Boschenmeer

In 1999, at the same time as the new 9 holes were added to the Paarl golf course, plots were introduced for sale in this sought after location. That this is a sought after location, is evident in the abundance of finished homes that now adorn this 140 hectare estate.

The ingredients for this success are easy to define. Apart from bordering the 27 hole golf course, the estate is in a splendid location only half an hour from Cape Town's city centre. This is the heart of the winelands, where mountain, river and vine blend into a scenic kaleidoscope of visual splendour. Famous wine estates offer food and wine choices for the palate and the nearby town of Franschhoek (known as the gourmet capital of the Cape) adds an array of restaurants, hotels, guest houses and shops to make the Boschenmeer resident work at decisions while enjoying the tranquil lifestyle on offer there.

Inside the secure, gated environment, the development of 'Estate Lodges' has provided a popular option to both local and overseas buyers. These are luxurious, fully furnished units available in two or four double bedroom options. Purchasers of these ideal 'lock up and go' properties have the added benefits of a golf cart and membership to the golf club.

A further benefit is that Boschenmeer is affiliated to The Interval International Exchange Programme. This exchange programme offers its members access to 1800 four and five star hotels and resorts in 70 countries worldwide.

11th hole

GRANDE ROCHE ★★★★★

PAARL

Set against the backdrop of a rugged mountain range and surrounded by ancient oaks and historic vineyards, the Grande Roche is only 40 minutes drive NE from Cape Town and its International Airport. A member of Relais & Chateaux, it epitomizes luxury, quiet elegance and romance. It features vine-clad Terrace- and historical Duplex Suites. Award-winning Bosman's Restaurant, Africa's only Relais Gourmand, has over many years garnered a deserved world-wide reputation.

***General Manager** Horst Frehse*
29 suites, 6 rooms, 2 swimming pools, gymnasium, tennis, massage, sauna and steam room.
Plantasie Street, Paarl. P.O. Box 6038, Paarl, 7622.
***phone** 021 863 2727* ***fax** 021 863 2220*
***e-mail** reserve@granderoche.com* ***website** www.granderoche.com*

PONTAC MANOR ★★★★

PAARL

Pontac Manor was formerly the Manor House on Pontac Estate, a wine estate founded in 1723. Surrounded by majestic oak trees, the manor has been restored to its former Victorian elegance, and the historic features in architecture and furnishings add charm and a sense of nostalgia for days gone by. Elegant rooms, informal lounges and tranquil gardens are further complemented by the well-deserved reputation of 'The Restaurant' at Pontac.

***General Manager** Sophie Barnard*
23 rooms, swimming pool, conference facilities.
16 Zion Street, Paarl, 7646.
***phone** 021 872 0445* ***fax** 021 872 0460*
***e-mail** pontac@iafrica.com* ***website** www.pontac.com*

PALMIET VALLEY ★★★★★

PAARL

The Palmiet Valley Estate is a working wine and fruit farm. In the heart of this tranquil environment is the historic manor house, built in 1692, that has been creatively restored by the estate's German owner. All bedrooms are en-suite with 4-Poster beds, fireplaces and thatched ceilings. Fine dining in the seventeenth-century dining room, or on the terrace under ancient oak trees, is supplemented by the estates own wines as well as those of the area.

Owner *Fred Uhlendorff*
10 rooms, swimming pool, restaurant
Klein Drakenstein. P.O. Box 9085, Klein Drakenstein, 7628, Paarl.
phone *021 862 7741* **fax** *021 862 6891*
e-mail *info@palmiet.co.za* **website** *www.palmiet.co.za*

ROGGELAND COUNTRY HOUSE

PAARL

The Cape Dutch farmhouse of Roggeland, rated one of the 50 best hotels in the world by Tatler Magazine, offers a 'complete country experience'. Enjoy superb regional cuisine partnered by the best local wines. Relaxed hospitality combine with an elegant ambience, tranquility and mountain views make for a wonderful stay. Roggeland is at the crossroads of four wine routes and six golf courses.

Owner *Gordon Minkley*
11 rooms, swimming pool.
Dal Josaphat, P.O. Box 7210, North Paarl, 7623.
phone *021 868 2501* **fax** *021 868 2113*
e-mail *rog@iafrica.com* **website** *www.roggeland.co.za*

MOUNTAIN SHADOWS ★★★

PAARL

Mountain Shadows is a historic manor house set amongst spectacular mountain scenery in the heart of the Cape wine country. This fine Cape Dutch house is a national monument dating back to 1823, and is the homestead of the estate developed in 1693 by an early Dutch settler, Herman Barentz. There are 13 double en-suite rooms and a delightful restaurant. The added bonus for the visiting golfer is the 6-hole 'golf course' situated in the back garden!

General Manager *Ian Taylorson*

13 rooms, swimming pool, conference facilities, 6 hole mashie course.

Klein Drakenstein Road P.O. Box 2501, Paarl, 7620.

phone *021 862 3192* ***fax*** *021 862 6796*

e-mail *mshadows@icon.co.za* ***website*** *www.mountainshadows.co.za*

LE QUARTIER FRANÇAIS ★★★★

FRANSCHHOEK

Le Quartier Français is a splash of style in the heart of the historic village of Franschhoek, a corner of the Cape Winelands that is a little France. Th standards begin in the spacious suites furnished with modern fittings, refreshing colours and brilliantly hand-painted fabrics, Egyptian cotton line and beautiful views. The restaurant has been voted in the top 50 restauran of the world by the reputable UK Restaurant magazine. Gould's special not Chef Margot Janse has been voted 'chef of the year' by 'Eat Out' magazin A Relais et Châteaux Hotel.

Owner *Susan Huxter*

15 air-conditioned luxury rooms, 2 luxury air-conditioned suites with private swimming pool and complimentary mini bars. Corner Berg and Wilhelmina Street, Franschhoek.

phone *021 876 2151* ***fax*** *021 876 3105*

e-mail *res@lqf.co.za* ***website*** *www.lequartier.co.za*

LA COURONNE HOTEL ★★★★★

FRANSCHHOEK

La Couronne is in one of the most unique settings in South Africa, neighboure by Mont Rochelle with vineyards high on a mountain overlooking the spectacul Franschhoek Valley. A tranquil ambience is reflected in the elegant bedrooms and suites and panoramic views of the area are available from the comfort of th gracious lounge and stylish restaurant. Enjoy the superb wine cellar amongst orchards and vineyards or walk in the private mountain forests.

Managing Director *Erwin Schnitzler*

17 Rooms (1 Pinotage suite, 8 Merlot rooms, 3 Shiraz rooms, 3 Chardonnay rooms ar 2 Sauvignon rooms) swimming pool, sauna, conference facilities.

Dassenburg Road, Franschhoek. P.O. Box 448, Franschhoek, 7690.

phone *021 876 2770/8* ***fax*** *021 876 3788*

e-mail *reservations@lacouronnehotel.co.za* ***website*** *www.lacouronnehotel.co.z*

WORCESTER

Worcester Golf Course

Length of Course: *5711 metres*

WORCESTER

Worcester Golf Course
Map reference: *33*
Length of Course: *5711 metres*
Holes: *18*
Type of Course: *Semi-desert*
Par: *72*
Visitors: *No restrictions*
Club Professional: *No*
Tuition: *Yes*
Club Shop: *Yes*
Practice Facilities: *Yes - own balls, putting green*
Hire Facilities: *Clubs, trollleys, caddies and drive carts*
Catering: *Bar, halfway house*
Location: *Kolie Nelson Drive, Worcester*
Contact: *Martin van Wyk*
Postal address: *P.O.Box 162, Worcester 6849*
Phone: *023 347 2542*
Fax: *023 347 5832*
e-mail: *worcgolf@mweb.co.za*
web: *www.wgc.com*

KAROO BUSH

The hills that nestle below the large and lengthy Brandwacht Mountain provide interesting terrain for the Worcester golf course, described as "Karoo Bush" because the fairways follow the contours around these hills and have been carved through Karoo Bush scrubland. This low, wiry bush now lines most of the fairways. As it is an undulating course, you will have some magnificent views of the area, its mountains and the town of Worcester.

Gary Player designed the course and that will give you an idea of its high standard. Some golfers (hookers and slicers in particular) describe the course as harsh, an adequate description, for, if you happen to stray off the more than adequately wide fairways, you will find yourself in bush and rock and will indeed be penalised. On the other hand, if you stay on the undulating fairways, you are assured of a really good golfing experience.

The course has had problems with the greens due to the prevailing dry conditions, but I am happy to report that ongoing improvements have resulted in these greens not detracting from this enjoyable challenge. A word of warning: January and February, Worcester can be unbearably hot, so choose your playing time carefully. A redeeming factor is that this is an ideal winter course and in August and September it is possible to play with snow on the Mountain tops, a carpet of wild flowers at your feet and sunshine on your back.

THE COURSE

5th Hole - Par 5 - 460 metres

A high elevated tee looks down on a fairway well below, which doglegs right. The Worcester scrubland protects the right and small trees and hillocks guard the other side of the fairway. This is a narrow fairway and tee shot placement is of prime importance. On reaching the green, you must avoid the dam on the left, which will necessitate aiming high right. Too long and you will have the company of a deep bunker halfway along the green. Too short will find you in a long flattish bunker. A big green, sloping uphill from front to back, is the target.

6th Hole - Par 4 - 307 metres

The only things visible from this tee are bush and water and you simply have to trust that after a 150-metre carry, there is a fairway. A word of warning - should your shot be too far left, you will meet the dam and, should your shot be too long, you will meet a water hazard that runs across the fairway.
This hole turns to the right, though your second shot will be straight to the green with what seems to be only a small bunker front right guarding it. There is however a second bunker on the far right to catch the "bail out" shot.

7th Hole - Par 3 - 138 metres

This is a great short hole with carry all the way over water. From the back tee the hole is 162 metres, while, from the front, it is only 120 metres. A solitary bunker protects the right middle, while sleepers curve around the front with the water gently lapping them. The views of the mountain backdrop, the rolling hills, the reeds around the dam and the ducks should add to the pleasure of clearing the water.

THE AREA

In recent years, this area has become the biggest wine-producing district in South Africa. The Madiba wine estate is worth visiting for, apart from its excellent wines, the modern cellar is of particular architectural interest.
For museum lovers, there are four to choose from and those of you keen on art should visit Hugo Naude House, built in 1904. This national monument currently serves as an art gallery and sculptures feature in the gardens. For another interesting step back into the past, you should visit the Kleinplasie open-air living museum which depicts the lifestyles of early pioneers. Here you may even learn how to roll tobacco, distill witblitz or bake bread in an outside oven.

CUMBERLAND HOTEL ★★★

WORCESTER

Egidio Cardoso, the long-term owner of this modern and superbly equipped hotel, has carved a well-deserved reputation in the hospitali industry. He has been a motivator in creating tours to the many touris attractions of the area. The hotel has 55 en-suite rooms, 2 restaurant 4 bars and if you require relaxation, you will find the leisure centre ide with its spa and sauna facilities. A sparkling central pool area allows f further relaxation and enjoyment.

Owner *Egidio Cardoso*
55 rooms, swimming pool, tennis, sauna and gymnasium. 2 Stockenstroom Street. P.O. Box 8, Worcester 6849
phone *023 347 2641* ***fax*** *023 347 3613*
e-mail *manager@cumberland.co.za* ***website*** *www.cumberland.co.za*

CHURCH STREET LODGE ★★

WORCESTER

The introduction of a reception counter adjoining the bar area, gives a warm and welcoming first impression at this hospitable lodge. Situate in the heart of Worcester, the rooms on offer are spacious and individual decorated. The swimming pool, fountains and quaint patios create a peaceful atmosphere, one that is well complemented by the committe personnel who will look after your every need.

Manager *Sue Kruger*
20 rooms, swimming pool
36 Church Street, Worcester, 6850.
phone *023 342 5194* ***fax*** *023 342 8859*
e-mail *manager@churchst.co.za* ***website*** *www.churchst.co.za*

DEVONVALE

Devonvale Golf Estate
Length of Course: *5705 metres*
Type of Course: *Parkland*
Holes: *18*
Par: *72*

DEVONVALE

Devonvale Golf Estate **Map reference:** 5
Length of Course: 5705 metres **Holes:** 18
Type of Course: Parkland **Par:** 72
Visitors: No restrictions
Club Professional: No
Tuition: On request **Club Shop:** Yes
Practice Facilities: Driving range, putting and chipping green, practice bunker
Hire Facilities: Clubs, trolleys, caddies and drive carts
Catering: Bar, restaurant, halfway house
Location: Bottelary Road, Koelenhof, Stellenbosch
Contact: Dominique Provoyeur
Postal address: P.O.Box 77, Koelenhof 7605
Phone reception: 021 865 2080 **Fax:** 021 865 2601
Phone proshop: 021 888 4735
e-mail: devonvale@intekom.co.za **web:** www.devonvale.co.za

HEAVEN VALE

The Devonvale Hotel and Conference Estate is set in a natural undulating valley, in the heart of the Stellenbosch winelands. The original design by a young Gary Player, was commissioned by Simeon Blumberg, who, over 40 years ago, foresaw the potential of developing real estate around a splendid golf course within easy reach of the centre of Cape Town. Zoning restrictions prevented this vision from being completed and, for many years, despite the quality of the golf course layout, Devonvale remained very much the country cousin to most of the more established and refined courses of this area.

Today, fortunately, the dream has been renovated and activated by J.J. Provoyeur and his partners and ably assisted by his daughter Dominique. JJ (as he is known in South Africa) is a former single-handed round the world sailor and the single-mindedness required for such a venture is now focused on establishing Devonvale as a sought after golf, hotel and real estate venue. In recent years, zoning rights have been lifted and the estate is now blessed with a real estate development, complementing the hotel and conference centre that are part of the splendid improvements to be enjoyed at this well established golf venue.

In order to ensure that the housing component would in no way interfere with the tranquillity and country feel of this scenic layout, the two finishing holes on the front nine have been re-designed. The 8th hole, formerly a tough and challenging par 3, has been transformed into a memorable par 4, curving around the large, central dam that is a feature on the course. The 9th, formerly a downhill par 4 to a green hugging the shores of the dam, is now a testing par 3. The green remains and the tee is equally close to the dam wall, so the test here is to ensure correct club selection and accuracy.

These changes apart, on the remainder of the course, new tees, wider tee boxes and the lengthening of many of the holes and the introduction of bent grass greens, are further additions. Apart from the aforementioned alterations, it hasn't been necessary to alter Mr Player's original design. Here, curving, sweeping fairways wind their way up and down a natural, rolling tree-lined land surrounded by mountains and vines.

13th hole

THE COURSE

2nd Hole - Par 5 - 455 metres

This hole begins from a high tee to a fairway below, which doglegs gently to the right. The landing area slopes quite sharply from left to right and a tee shot too far right will run down a steep embankment. On reaching this green consideration of the pin placement is all-important as the surface slopes steeply from right to left.

3rd Hole - Par 5 - 453 metres

It is unusual to enjoy two par 5's in a row. This hole is challenging off the tee as a row of trees on the right and out of bounds vineyards on the left make for an intimidating tee shot. There is some respite however, as the fairway widens and runs downhill to a large green that slopes uphill from front to back. Any shot overshooting this target will have a steep embankment to negotiate on the way back to the green.

4th Hole - Par 4 - 328 metres

This hole is noteworthy for its beautiful mountain backdrop. It features a sharp dogleg to the left and the prudent shot is to stay to the right of the fairway. The longer hitters will skirt with out of bounds to the left and cut the corner. A water hazard can come into play though if the shot is too far left. There is another water hazard short and to the right of the elevated green. This green also slopes from right to left but there is a margin for error before reaching the green.

9th hol

4th ho

THE ESTATE

The property development introduced to Devonvale offers completed two-storey homes, situated on stands between 180 and 700 square metres in size. The chosen architectural theme has been described as 'English Country' style and the earthy colours and the dark roofs with variable patterns blend well into the landscape. The housing development situated on high ground above the course, allows for splendid views of the countryside, and when completed will have 80 properties. The home-owners and the hotel guests will avail themselves of not only the golf course facility but, in the not too distant future, they will be able to sample the wines from the Devonvale vineyards. On suitable land on the borders of the estate, vines have been planted and this will allow future residents, golfers and conference delegates alike to savour the Devonvale Golf Estate Wines. To understand that this is the ideal wine growing area, the visitor has just to turn right out of the secure, gated environment and follow the uphill road to capture one of the most marvellous of views over the Devon Valley. The imposing Simonsberg Mountain stands proudly in the distance while in the valley below, vines creep on, around and below the gentle slopes that provide the harvest of some of South Africa's champion wines.

Gould's special note:

This view over Devon Valley is majestic. I took Juan Espi (who produces the wonderful photographs for this guide) to see the view for the first time. On seeing all the wine estates below he was to wax lyrically -"Wow - Heaven Vale - The valley of a thousand bottles!" He spent the next two hours capturing the sensational scenery on film.

ONS GENOT ★★★★

STELLENBOSCH

This exclusive country retreat on the outskirts of the Cape Winelands was a finalist in the Accommodation Awards in 2002. The luxury en-suite air-conditioned rooms have a private terrace leading to an attractiv garden setting, while the Honeymoon Suite has a private jacuzzi. Ther is a cosy lounge with an open fire and an inviting dining area where a 'champagne breakfast is served. Your hosts Marleen and Eric, will provide for your every need and can converse in several languages!

Owners *Marleen and Eric Bovijn*
9 rooms, swimming pool, tennis court, secure parking.
Bottelary Road, Stellenbosch. P.O. Box 163, Koelenhof, 7605.
phone *021 865 2233* ***fax*** *021 865 2250*
e-mail *info@onsgenot.com* ***website*** *www.onsgenot.com*

WEDGEVIEW COUNTRY HOUSE ★★★★★

STELLENBOSCH

This beautiful thatched property is set on over four acres of stunning gardens, surrounded by vineyards with spectacular views of the Stellenbosch mountains Hosts, Mike and Trudie Spicer, from England, welcome you to their lovely home where the king sized beds, in the spacious and luxurious bedrooms, are enhance by fine linen, with feather down pillows and duvets. Relax by the pool, play a game of snooker, savour the fine malt whiskies from the bar, or simply enjoy the fine ambience of the house.

Owners *Mike and Trudie Spicer*
9 rooms, swimming pool, jacuzzi, snooker room, drawing room, sitting room, expansive quiet gardens. P.O. Box 62, The Bonniemile, Vlottenburg 7604 near Stellenbosch.
phone *021 8813525* ***cell*** *082 853 2374* ***fax*** *021 8813539*
e-mail *wedgeview@adept.co.za* ***website*** *www.wedgeview.co.za*

STELLENBOSCH

Stellenbosch Golf Course
Length of Course: *6535 metres*
Type of Course: *Parkland*
Holes: *18*
Par: *74*

STELLENBOSCH

Stellenbosch Golf Course | **Map reference:** 30
Length of Course: 6535 metres | **Holes:** 18
Type of Course: Parkland | **Par:** 74
Visitors: Wednesday afternoon and Saturday reserved for members
Club Professional: Arnold Mentz 021 880 0244
Tuition: Yes | **Club Shop:** Yes
Practice Facilities: Driving range, putting greens
Hire Facilities: Clubs, trolleys, caddies and drive carts
Catering: Bar, restaurant, halfway house and snacks
Location: Strand Road, Stellenbosch
Manager: Kobus Du Toit
Postal address: P.O.Box 277, Stellenbosch, 7599
Phone: 021 880 0103 | **Fax:** 021 880 0260
e-mail: bookings.stellenbosch@mweb.co.za

SNAKES AND GRAPES

As you approach the University town of Stellenbosch, you will notice the Simonsberg Mountain that forms an imposing backdrop for this picturesque town. Legend has it that the mountain is actually the sleeping form of Simon Van Der Stel (after whom Stellenbosch was named) and that, should he ever be awakened; the town would face serious problems. I cannot help but think that Mr Van Der Stel has one eye sneakily opened to peek at the majestic scenery that surrounds this historical town, for, who could sleep through such beauty? His gaze will also, no doubt, fall on the beautiful tree-lined fairways of the Stellenbosch Golf Club, surrounded by mountain slopes under vine.

Although the tree-lined fairways may be intimidating at first, because of the sometimes narrow framework in which to play from tee to green, you will soon realise how much room there actually is if you follow a clever game plan.

In 1999 Stellenbosch hosted the South African Open Championship and several improvements were made, including new water hazards at the 12th and 18th holes. In the ensuing years, under the guidance of a vibrant new committee, course improvements continue. Apart from these, you will find Stellenbosch much as it has always been and, as I'm sure you will agree, there is not much to improve on what nature has provided in the heart of this wineland area.

The clubhouse has also been substantially upgraded and it is worth enjoying the 19th hole on the terrace to savour the surrounding Mountain scenery.

Gould's Special Note:
The 1999 winner of the South African Open at Stellenbosch was South African golfer David Frost, who in his younger days was a regular player on this course. As I was privileged to play with him several times - I was delighted to see he hadn't forgotten what I taught him!

THE COURSE

6th Hole - Par 4 - 375 metres

This is a difficult hole with a vineyard to the left of the fairway and the green perched up on a hill behind. Your drive should preferably be down the left middle of the fairway. The green sits well above the fairway and is protected by trees fronting it and a steep bank front and left. Club selection is all-important to ensure a carry all the way to the target. Anything hit short and left will run back towards the vines and out of bounds.

7th Hole - Par 3 - 130 metres

This is the shortest hole on the course but it is certainly not the easiest. The green is wide with a severe bunker at the front stretching from the middle to the right hand side. It is positioned at the bottom of a hill and requires no more than an eight or nine iron in order to carry the tee shot all the way. Anything hit short will bounce forward through the green where bunkers will stop the ball from running out of bounds.

8th Hole - Par 5 - 440 metres

This hole is known to the locals as "Snakes and Grapes"- snakes to the right in the thick bush and grapes growing in the vineyards to the left. The fairway slopes steeply from right to left and the tee shot should be played to the high right in order for the ball to finish in the middle. The second is likely to be above the feet and care must be taken against a pull shot back to the vines. At the green, there is a deep bunker to the left and the green itself slopes uphill. It is prudent to leave the approach shot below the pin.

THE AREA

A visit to the 315 year-old town of Stellenbosch should not be missed. History and modernity blend well in this town which houses over 16 000 students. A guided walking tour is definitely the best way to see the town. A R10 investment at the Tourist Office will take you on a pleasant stroll under the oaks past the Modderkerk down Dorp Street, South Africa's second oldest street, to the Braak and past many historical and beautiful buildings.

This is the heart of the winelands and you can visit a multitude of wine estates and enjoy tastings. Most of the estates offer lunches and organised cellar tours.

My personal favourites are Delaire (for the view!) and Thelema (for the wine!).

SUMMERWOOD ★★★★★

STELLENBOSCH

Enjoy the tranquility of this meticulously restored private mansion dating fro 1903, with its beautiful grounds and large pool. Tastefully furnished and equipped en-suite rooms, guest lounge and sunny breakfast room leadin out onto a terrace, provide every comfort. Summerwood is just a short str from the historic centre of Stellenbosch and only ten minutes drive from Devon Vale, De Zalze & Stellenbosch golf courses. Hilary and Malcolm delight in helping their guests appreciate this special corner of South Afric

Owner and Managers *Hilary and Malcolm Forbes*
9 rooms, swimming pool. 28 Jonkershoek Road, Stellenbosch, 7600.
phone *021 887 4112* **fax** *021 887 4239*
e-mail *summerwood@mweb.co.za* **website** *www.summerwood.co.za*

RIVER MANOR

STELLENBOSCH

Across from the Eerste River, in a peaceful avenue of oak trees, Rive Manor is two minutes stroll from the charming village centre. The histor River Manor combines "colonial charm with touches of Africa". Elegar rooms have the added luxury of fresh flowers, port and sherry trays an plush bathrobes. Enjoy a leisurely poolside breakfast, or indulge yours at the intimate health and beauty spa in a secluded garden. Johan an Leigh are your gracious hosts.

Owners *Leigh and Johan Swanepoel*
16 rooms, 2 swimming pools, health and beauty spa.
6 The Avenue, Stellenbosch, 7600.
tel *021 887-9944* **fax** *021 887-9940*
e-mail *rivermanor@adept.co.za* **website** *www.rivermanor.com*

D'OUWE WERF ★★★★

STELLENBOSCH

This country inn, in one of the most historic buildings in South Africa, has had a reputation for outstanding hospitality since 1802. The hotel has an excellent restaurant on the premises, which serves traditional dishes from the Cape region. Staying in such an old building you might expect 'olde worlde' décor – and you will not be disappointed when you see the splendid antiques, rich wood finishes and soft mellow fabrics.

Owner and Manager *Cobus Venter*
25 rooms, swimming pool, airconditioning, free parking
30 Church Street, Stellenbosch, 7600.
phone *021 887 4608* ***fax*** *021 887 4626*
e-mail *ouwewerf@iafrica.com* ***website*** *www.ouwewerf.com*

BONNE ESPERANCE

STELLENBOSCH

John and Sue Savage have carefully restored this Victorian home and the result is a charming guest lodge. All the guest rooms have been individually decorated and the dining room, with its butter-yellow decor, is a pleasant environment in which to enjoy breakfast before a rigorous day on the golf course. The restful courtyard garden features a plunge pool that beckons one in the hot summer months.

Owners *John and Sue Savage*
15 guest rooms, plunge pool.
17 Van Riebeeck Street, Stellenbosch 7600, Cape of Good Hope.
tel *021 887 0225* ***fax*** *021 887 8328*
e-mail *stay@bonneesperance.com* ***website*** *www.bonneesperance.com*

DE ZALZE

De Zalze Golf Estate

Length of Course: *5937 metres*

DE ZALZE

De Zalze Golf Estate **Map reference:** *28*
Length of Course: *5937 metres* **Holes:** *18*
Type of Course: *Parkland* **Par:** *72*
Visitors: *No restrictions*
Club Professional: *None*
Tuition: *None (opening soon The Frost golf Acadamy at De Zalze)*
Club Shop: *Yes*
Practice Facilities: *None at present (opening October 2003)*
Hire Facilities: *Clubs, trolleys and drive carts*
Catering: *Restaurant, halfway house*
Location: *Off the R44-turn into the Kleine Zalze Wine Estate.*
Contact: *Lance Hurley*
Postal address: *P.O.Box 12706, Die Boord, Stellenbosch*
Phone: *021 880 1996* **Fax:** *021 880 1976*
e-mail: *info@spiergolf.co.za* **web:** *www.spier.co.za*

MATURING IN THE WINELANDS

The De Zalze Country Club opened in the latter part of 2000. The golf course forms part of the splendid multi-faceted Spier estate and the Peter Matkovich design has added another quality product to the De Zalze collection of amenities.

This is a course that immediately received high praise for its layout in the midst of working vineyards and orchards. The Stellenbosch mountain range acts as constant backdrop, adding to the reputation the course has gained for its scenic surrounds. Since its opening, much has been done to mature the course to perfection. On opening, several telephone poles impeded play on the beginning holes but these will be history as the development of a real estate component is being implemented. A temporary clubhouse, situated in the Cellars of the Kleine Zalze wine estate, adds a memorable charm to the aura of this winelands golf course. The 'temporary home' will give way to a permanent clubhouse destined to be housed at the centre of the golf course and this will result in a change of the numbering of the holes.

What will remain constant are the superb holes set on rolling and undulating terrain. These meander between grape on the vine, fruit on the tree and an array of superb water features, the most memorable being the lake that borders the 10th, 11th and 12th holes. Peter Matkovich is well known for his motto 'Listen to the Land' and here he truly was in listening mode, as he has captured the many moods of this area. Like its wine counterpart on its borders, this course will mature in years to become one of South Africa's leading golf venues.

THE COURSE

Already in place are the superb Kikuyu fairways and large bent grass greens, all with the Matkovich trademark of finely manicured aprons. Many who play this course will forever remember the 12th hole, where from an island tee, a high risk shot over water will allow this par 4 green to be reached in one. However, accuracy is at a premium to avoid a watery grave. The more prudent players will aim for the curving fairway lined by tall pines and sandy hazards. The moods to enjoy here are the fairways lined by vineyards and those fairways lined by orchards. Tall pines, river crossings, and elevated tees, as well as the myriad of sparkling water features are further pleasures. All of these are complemented by the mountain surrounds of this beautiful area of the Cape.

Gould's special note:

At the time of writing, the course is set up to begin from the temporary clubhouse at the Kleine Zalze wine estate that borders the course. In time to come, the clubhouse will be moved to overlook the current 17th and 18th holes and the current 9th tee. The configuration of the holes will alter when the new clubhouse is completed.

11th hole

2nd Hole - Par 3 - 145 metres

This is a truly picturesque par 3 hole. There is carry over a rocky-river crossing and the entrance is framed by trees. The green, while well protected by bunkers, curves around a grassy mound. If the pin is to the right careful thought on club selection and ball position will be required.

3rd Hole - Par 4 - 374 metres

This stroke 1 hole has a wide fairway that narrows where a thicket of trees left and a rocky mound right impinge two thirds of the way. Only a bunker back left is to be avoided at the green. This green slopes uphill from front to back and from left to right.

7th Hole - Par 5 - 467 metres

The first time visitor will note this is a blind tee shot that obviously requires threading the fairway bunkers. At the landing area off the tee, the fairway sweeps sharply downhill and gently left to an intimidating target guarded by water, and a high grassy bank to the left and several sand traps to the right. The longer hitters will have the high-risk high-reward option as this downhill hole is reachable in two. My advice is caution first!

16th Hole - Par 5 - 514 metres

This is one of the toughest par five holes in the Cape! The fairway curves to the left of a high, grassy mound and straightens back to the hole. It is prudent to remain left, where the second shot needs to remain short of river crossing the fairway before the green. There is a high, grassy bank fronting this elevated green and anything short will find a rolling path back to water. The green sits high above the fairway and the degree of difficulty is enhanced by the river running to the right of it.

SPIER ESTATE

Spier offers a kaleidoscope of recreation, food and wine facilities and entertainment for both the day visitor and those looking to stay for a while longer. The 'Village Hotel' provides a calm and tranquil environment for the overnight guest. The 155 bedrooms of the hotel are housed in 32 separate double-storey buildings. A river frontage and natural winding paths create the 'Village' feel, while inside the main central building the spacious welcoming lobby leads via Toto's bar to the beautifully decorated bistro restaurant, Figaros. Toto's bar and the restaurant are both fronted by a sunny terrace, allowing for restful moments to savour the scenic surrounds of the mountain ranges.

Those guests not wishing to take advantage of the swimming pool surrounds or to lounge in the tasteful relaxation of the bedrooms will find much to do on the doorstep of the hotel. An array of restaurants, riverside and lakeside picnic areas and a farmstall provide ample choices for relaxing dining experiences. The Jonkershuis restaurant, housed in a 150 year old building, is a personal favourite, as it offers a unique taste of spicy Cape Malay foods. The colourful presentation of the food is as memorable as the exotic tastes on offer. There are several quality retail outlets, also housed in historical environments. The Cape Weavers centre, the Danieel Diamond

centre and the Spier shop all serve to provide the ideal memorabilia of South Africa or the perfect thoughtful gift.

The Spier Wine Centre is a haven for the winelover. The cellar is housed in a gabled barn that dates back to 1856, and the treasures to be found here require some concentration as there is an abundance of quality and variety of choice.

Spier has truly managed to blend the sense of history with today's modern requirements. This is reflected when you have visited the carefully restored Manor House, built in 1884, and then you attend one of the spectacular entertainment events that are regularly held in the modern open-air theatre. The Spier Summer Arts Festival has become part of Cape Town's social calendar. If you are visiting when this festival is on, you will be assured of experiencing exceptional local and international artists, all under a dazzling African sky.

For the more energetic there are tennis courts. These are part of a Tennis Academy and the floodlit arena has been host to an exhibition match between Anna Kournikova and our own Amanda Koetzee. The visit to this remarkable estate would not be complete without visiting the Cheetah Park, where land has been made available to a group of hand-reared cheetahs as part of the Cheetah Out-Reach programme. There is also an opportunity to get up close and personal with eagles. Eagles Encounter is run by Hank and Tracy Chalmers, experts in their field. You will marvel at the majesty and power of a variety of eagles.

Gould's special note:

I have always been impressed by the environmental and social responsibility of the Spier developers. Every aspect has included sharing with the local community and ensuring sustainable development of the area and the people.

DE ZALZE WINELANDS ESTATE

While many visit Spier to 'stay for a while', soon there will be an opportunity to savour a more permanent lifestyle on this estate set in the heart of the Stellenbosch winelands. On the scenic sloping landscape that borders the Spier Country Club and the Kleine Zalze wine estate, services are being laid to introduce a housing development. The development of individual village clusters, collectively housing in the region of 500 plots, is in progress as I write, and it is a testament to the popularity of this location that even before any marketing has been implemented, 130 plots have been sold.

L'AVENIR WINE ESTATE ★★★

STELLENBOSCH

L'Avenir is situated in the heart of the Winelands. Set in the foothills of the Simonsberg Mountains, the Guest House is surrounded by 70 hectares of splendid vineyards, the wine a tribute to the art of winemaking. Nine guest suites, colonial charm, warm hospitality and personalized service are jewels set in Stellenbosch's crown of historical, cultural and culinary beauty. Here, "regular guests" have found its true meaning.

Manager *Ann Homola*
9 rooms, swimming pool, conference room, close to golf courses
Klapmuts Road. P.O. Box 1135, Stellenbosch, 7599.
phone *021 889 5001* ***fax*** *021 889 7313*
e-mail *lavenirguesthouse@absamail.co.za* ***website*** *www.lavenir.co.za*

EIKENDAL LODGE ★★★★

STELLENBOSCH

Eikendal Lodge is situated in the heart of its own luscious vineyards. Splendid views of the surrounding mountains and scenic countryside are available from the private terraces of the en-suite bedrooms. The lodge is famed for its hearty breakfasts served in the elegant breakfast room or open-air terrace that leads to landscaped gardens and a sparkling pool. The Eikendal wine cellar offers the chance to taste premium wines and enjoy a light lunch.

General Manager *Leonie Fourie*
9 rooms, swimming pool, wine cellar.
Eikendal Road, Stellenbosch. P.O. Box 2261 Dennesig, Stellenbosch, 7601.
phone *021 855 3617* ***fax*** *021 855 3862*
e-mail *lodge@eikendal.com* ***website*** *www.eikendal.com*

SOMERSET WEST

Somerset West Golf Course

Length of Course: *5928 metres*

SOMERSET WEST

Somerset West Golf Course **Map reference:** *27*
Length of Course: *5928 metres* **Holes:** *18*
Type of Course: *Parkland* **Par:** *73*
Visitors: *Booking essential for weekends*
Club Professional: *Chester Visser 021 852 3625*
Tuition: *Yes* **Club Shop:** *Yes*
Practice Facilities: *Putting greens*
Hire Facilities: *Clubs, trolleys, caddies and drive carts*
Catering: *Bar, restaurant, halfway house*
Club Manager: *Ryk Myburgh*
Address: *Rue de Jacqueline, Somerset West 7130*
Phone: *021 852 2925* **Fax:** *021 852 5879*
e-mail: *swgc@hixnet.co.za* **web:** *www.somersetwestgolfclub.co.za*

A TRUE COUNTRY CLUB

Whilst playing this parkland course you will cross a railway line and a road on what is essentially a golf course of three different parts, but in no way does that change its feeling or style.

As you play, look out for the white squirrels that live around the first nine holes. Whilst throughout the Cape you'll find grey squirrels, these little fellows are quite special.

This is not only a golf club but, being a true Country Club; it also offers tennis, bowls and squash as leisure facilities.

In winter the area can be very wet and you are advised to check conditions when you book to play. One thing is certain, you will enjoy the 19th Hole as the bar here provides a warm, friendly atmosphere and you will find the members most welcoming.

Gould's note:

I once played a few holes here with Gary Player. At the 16th hole there is a bunker on the right. Mr. Player - to me he's Mr. Player - took time out to show my partners and me how to play out of this bunker to a flag at the back of the green. He dropped three balls into the sand. The first ball he hit two inches from the flag; and then he sank the next two! Awesome. All he told us was: "That's how to play that shot. Good luck!"

THE COURSE

12th Hole - Par 5 - 470 metres

A wide expanse of fairway will tempt you to a big drive, but beware the reeded dam that runs along the right of the fairway. The fairway narrows as a left hand dam comes into play and the second shot has to be hit over a water hazard connecting the two dams. As the hole turns gently to the right it is best to bear left as the green has a slope from right to left with a bunker protecting the right.

13th Hole - Par 3 - 147 metres

This is a demanding short hole as no less than four bunkers surround the green - two right and two left. The gap between them is narrow and you will be required to carry the ball all the way. The backdrop of trees will caution you against over-clubbing.

14th Hole - Par 4 - 363 metres

This is a majestic par 4. In the distance the Hottentots Holland Mountains provide a backdrop to tall flat-topped pines. Two large trees on either side of the fairway make for a narrow perspective to what is, in fact, a wide landing area. The real test is with the second shot, for just past the fairway mound, with a weeping willow to the right, there is a wide water hazard carry. Although the green is some distance past this, the short hitter might prefer to lay up short of the water. Gentle slopes right and left on the green will nestle the ball back to its flat centre.

THE AREA

Somerset West is a starting point of the Stellenbosch Wine Route and here you will find excellent estates to visit.

Up the valley, along Lourensford Road, is the historic Vergelegen Wine Estate. Laid out in 1699 along the Lourens River by the wealthy Willem Adriaan van der Stel, expert agronomist and third Governor of the Cape, this residence is a significant heritage. Not only are the grand buildings charming for their Cape Dutch style, or curious as old slave quarters, but in the generous park-like setting, enormous camphor trees planted nearly 300 years ago by the governor, are also National Monuments. Lunch in this setting, under the dappled shade, is a treat.

On the road to Stellenbosch is Avontuur, renowned as a producer of excellent wines and as a horse stud-farm. You'll be welcomed at its wine tasting centre.

Nearby is the Auberge du Paysan Restaurant, one of the gems of fine dining. It's â la carte menu offers dishes made from the bountiful fresh farm produce of the area, and complemented by the best of local wines.

SÉRÉNITÉ
WELLNESS CENTRES | South Africa

SÉRÉNITÉ
| CONSTANTIA

...TUCKED AWAY AMONG THE LUSH FORESTS OF TH CAPE'S CONSTANTIA VALLEY, THE SÉRÉNITÉ CONSTANTI GENTLY ENFOLDS EACH VISITOR WITH A SENSE OF SERENIT AND WELL-BEING...

...open your eyes,
saturate your senses,
awaken your spirit and experience the
wonderful feeling of overall wellness

Our signature treatments include:

- Sérénité Total Wellness Experience Massage (2hrs)
- An outdoor massage in our famous meditation sanctuary overlooking the Cape Winelands.
- Synchronised Massage (2 Therapists Synchronising Massage Movement) (1hr)
- Marine Detox Experience

STRAND

Strand Golf Course

Length of Course: *5732 metres*

STRAND

Strand Golf Course **Map reference:** *31*
Length of Course: *5732 metres* **Holes:** *18*
Type of Course: *Parkland* **Par:** *72*
Visitors: *Advisable to book on Wednesdays and Saturdays*
Club Professional: *Francois Van Den Bos 021 854 3309*
Tuition: *Yes* **Club Shop:** *Yes*
Practice Facilities: *Putting greens, driving range (own balls)*
Hire Facilities: *Clubs, trolleys, caddies and drive carts*
Catering: *Bar, restaurant, halfway house*
Location: *Beach Road, Strand*
Contact: *Cornie Blom*
Postal address: *P.O.Box 27, Strand 7140*
Phone: *021 853 6268* **Fax:** *021 854 6281*
e-mail: *stragolf@iafrica.com*

COASTAL SPLENDOUR

This is one of the Cape's newest additions to the golfing circuit. The course opened in 1994 and the championship layout has proved to be an exciting challenge for any golfer. In the intervening years, the course has matured greatly and a feature has been the attention given to the manicuring and maintenance of the surrounds. This is immediately noticeable from the upstairs terrace of the modern clubhouse as you look over the finishing hole and note the manicured surrounds of the sparkling water features.

The prominent features of the course are the abundant water hazards and bunkers, undulating greens and tree-lined fairways.

Right from the opening, the bent grass greens provided excellent putting surfaces and this remains a fact several years later. There are several tee boxes on each hole, which makes for a five hundred metre difference between championship tees and club tees over the 18 holes. In 1994, two and a half thousand trees were planted on this course and they are now becoming very much part of the round. There are still some open areas where the wind will be a factor. This is especially so as the course is situated close to the popular holiday coastal town of the Strand. This area, famed for its long stretch of unspoilt beach, does have a reputation for blustery conditions at certain times of the year. However, this will not detract from the experience to be enjoyed here.

THE COURSE

2nd Hole - Par 5 - 431 metres

This hole features a slight dogleg right and then left with the fairway meandering through an avenue of trees. There is a large tree on the right that encroaches on the fairway and your tee shot, aimed at a narrow target, should be just to the left of this tree. A river runs along the left side of the fairway and long hitters will go over the aforementioned tree with a drive and probably a 4 iron through the gap. For the less ambitious, it is a lay up to the narrow gap with a short iron to the green.

3rd Hole - Par 3 - 128 metres

Here, you are hitting a short iron to a green protected by a cloverleaf-shaped bunker on the left and the trees and river fronting the tee should not pose a problem. Problems, however, will arise if your shot is too far left into the trees or if it is too long or to the right where your ball will roll away on the undulating slopes guarding the green. If you are playing from the back tees, the hole becomes 185 metres and a completely different prospect.

4th Hole - Par 4 - 222 metres

This hole is short but don't be misled into thinking that you can relax because it really is a tight driving hole. You will be hitting an iron for placement and you will have to hit it straight. Low bush and brush guard either side of the narrow fairway before the fairway takes a slight turn to the left. The second shot is to a narrow green that is protected by a back bunker and a bunker front right. You can drive the green!

THE AREA

Both Gordon's Bay and the Strand are popular holiday resorts as they boast long, white beaches and warm waters in which to swim. The beaches in these areas slope gently into the sea making it possible to wade out for distances up to 100m, especially when the tide is low.

Gordon's Bay started life as a fishing village and today, the small harbour is still filled with fishing boats as well as yachts and speedboats. Canoeing in the Bay on calm days is a popular pastime and sea cruises from the harbour are available. It is well worth making some time to take a drive up the coast from Gordon's Bay towards magnificent spots such as Dappat se Gat and Koeelbaai where you will enjoy spectacular views.

LORD CHARLES HOTEL ★★★★

SOMERSET WEST

Golden Tulip The Lord Charles hotel has earned a deserved reputation as one of the Cape's finest hotels. This reputation has affected to both the leisure and the conference markets, as this hotel is ideally suited to both. Rich, warm and tasteful décor adorns both the en-suite rooms and the public areas, and there are an abundance of facilities to choose from. Fine dining in the La Vigna, and a visit to the aptly named St Andrews 19th, hole are my recommendations!

General Manager *Johan Agricola*
188 air-conditioned rooms, 9 luxury suites, 2 swimming pools, tennis, conference facilities
c/o Faure and Stellenbosch Roads, Somerset West. P.O. Box 5151, Helderberg, 7130
phone *021 855 1040* ***fax*** *021 855 1107*
e-mail *info@the-lord-charles.co.za* ***website*** *www.the-lord-charles.co.za*

STRAND BEACH HOTEL ★★★★

GORDONS BAY

This exciting 100 all-suite hotel, only 35 minutes from Cape Town, and only 20 minutes from the airport, overlooks the Strand warm water beachfront, on what is fast becoming known as the Sapphire Coast. Luxurious 3 bedroomed, 3 bathroom Penthouses are a feature, while the sweeping seascapes of the whole of False Bay from Cape Point to Table Mountain are truly memorable. The 'Original Fishmonger Restaurant offers fine fare and fine atmosphere.

Executive Chairman *Edmond Fenton*
98 rooms, 2 penthouse suites, swimming pool, conference facilities
17 Beach Road, Strand, 7139. P.O. Box 490, Strand, 7139
phone *021 850 9400* ***fax*** *021 850 9555*
e-mail *reservations@strandbeach.co.za* ***website*** *www.sapphiregroup.co.za*

ERINVALE

Erinvale Golf Estate

Length of Course: *5892 metres*

Type of Course: *Parkland*

Holes: *18*

Par: *72*

ERINVALE

Erinvale Golf Estate ***Map reference:*** *7*
Length of Course: *5892 metres* ***Holes:*** *18*
Type of Course: *Parkland* ***Par:*** *72*
Visitors: *Private Club - booking essential*
Director of Golf: *Bruce Bain 021 847 1906*
Tuition: *Yes* ***Club Shop:*** *Yes*
Practice Facilities: *Driving range, putting green, chipping green*
Hire Facilities: *Clubs, trolleys, no caddies and drive carts*
Catering: *Bar, halfway house*
Location: *Lourensford Road, Somerset West*
Contact: *Brian Cousins*
Postal address: *P.O.Box 3500, Somerset West 7129*
Phone: *021 847 1144* ***Fax:*** *021 847 1070*
e-mail: *clubhouse@erinvale.com* ***web:*** *www.erinvale.com*

SCENIC SPLENDOUR

In 1996, Erinvale Golf Estate hosted the World Cup of Golf. A world-wide TV audience and over 84 000 local spectators witnessed South Africa's Ernie Els and Wayne Westner achieve an incredible victory on home soil. In 2003, more drama will unfold on this scenically splendid golf arena as the South African Airways Open will be played there for the first time.

Once again, an international TV audience will marvel at the sensational vistas on and around the finishing stretch of this golf course of two very different moods. The first nine holes are built on flat terrain with challenging holes made more difficult by strategic water hazards and an array of different style bunkers. These sand traps range from traditional, large, well shaped bunkers, to some with railway sleepers and sandy slopes. Sod bunkers (as seen at the 17th hole at St Andrews) that are challenging, yet aesthetically pleasing, complete the picture.

The second nine holes are on undulating high ground. Here the scenic splendour might distract the players from the continuing challenge. Once again, water and bunkers are the main features with the added test of sloping lies.

The greens at Erinvale are huge and well shaped, allowing for several different pin placements. A feature of the layout is that different coloured flags tell you the pin position. Red flags at the back, yellow in the middle and white at the front. In most cases it will be important to note this, as there can be a two or three club difference between front and back

pin positions.
Erinvale is also a highly sought after real estate development. On both nines, homes adorn the fairways and the hilly landscape on offer, while many are fortunate to have dam frontages to add to the remarkable views available to the lucky permanent inhabitant.
In the intervening years between the World Cup and the South African Airways Open, the club has enjoyed fine tuning of its already splendid facilities. The clubhouse has been tastefully extended and a Koi fish pond is a memorable aspect inside the entrance. A must do, during your visit here, is to take time to sit on the outside terraces, either downstairs or upstairs, to savour the truly magnificent mountain surrounds. Catch them in the late evening light and the majesty of nature's colours will be forever imprinted on your mind.

Gould's special note:
This is my home club and I know you will receive a warm welcome. Though beware - mention my name and they may charge you double!

THE COURSE

Gary Player was the designer of the course and little of his immaculate challenge has been altered. The introduction of trees and the considerable care of manicuring the surrounds are nevertheless noticeable improvements
The first nine holes are on the low, flat part of the estate and the second nine are on high, undulating ground. This will give you two different feels, but there remains a common thread - that is the standard of the superbly shaped greens, with truly consistent putting surfaces. The 1st hole, a dogleg right, epitomises the Erinvale experience. You can choose a safe line straight off the tee leaving a long second to an elevated green well protected by bunkers and water to the right. The

more ambitious will cut the corner with their drive. This requires a carry over water and a ditch, as well as the avoidance of trees. The reward is a short iron to a difficult target.

Throughout the course there are majestic mountain backdrops, panoramic views of the surrounding hillsides planted with vine and sparkling views of the ocean from the higher vantage points.

Clubhouse

I have chosen to describe the finishing holes on both nines. These are excellent holes. However, I assure you that the experience and scenery around the other 16 will be cherished by the participants in the South African Airways Open as well as those of you who get to play on this superb layout in the winelands.

9th Hole - Par 4 - 365 metres

From the tee you are required to avoid five deep bunkers on the left. The fairway, quite wide but out of bounds, awaits you on the right. The second requires a long, precise iron or wood (depending on your skill) to a narrow target fronted by a rocky stream that also follows the left of this very long green.

18th Hole - Par 4 - 356 metres

This is a superb finishing hole! The modern clubhouse directly behind the 18th is your target. You will be required to deviate left of the five bunkers (the same ones as on the 9th) off the tee. You will then be required to find the right club to reach a massive green surrounded by four bunkers of differing size and depth. Here it is important to check the pin placement on this quite majestic green as it could make a four club difference.

The feature hole at Erinvale is the short par 3, 8th hole. However, my personal favourite is the downhill par 4, 17th hole which I would feature in any list of great golf holes. An out of bounds fence runs alongside the fairway on the right and tall pines accompany the left. An accurate drive will reach a fairway running steeply downhill and longer hitters will take advantage of this. For the average golfer, a long second shot is required to negotiate a narrowing fairway leading to a surprisingly small green, protected by severe bunkers on either side. The green itself needs concentration as it has some severe slopes to test the putter. This is especially so if the pin is on the right.

Gould's special note:

There are no caddies at Erinvale and drive carts are recommended- especially for the undulating second nine.

9th hole

9th hole

8th hole

ERINVALE HOTEL

Just outside the gated environment of the estate is the Erinvale Estate Hotel. This charming thatched property will no doubt house the players and management of the South African Airways Open. These participants will be enchanted by the historical buildings that are set under splendid trees and surrounded by the majestic Hottentots Holland Mountains. The welcome is in the original thatched manor house and the rooms are in the original stables that have been charmingly converted into comfortable en-suite bedrooms. A newer bedroom wing is decorated in the traditional Cape style.

The dining experience at the hotel has two equally compelling venues, each with a different mood. The more formal Blaskets restaurant offers fine fare, while the casual atmosphere of the popular Skelling's pub is sought after for its traditional dishes. The hotel has gained a deserved reputation for its conference and wedding facilities. A delightful chapel adds to the romantic atmosphere and a sparkling swimming pool area and well maintained gardens are additional features.

Gould's special note:

I once took a group of 55 French golfers to stay at the hotel. By the first night, stocks of quality red wine had been severely depleted. It is a testament to the service here that by the second night, we were offered an array of choice that had obviously been hastily collected from the many nearby estates. We have been repeat customers ever-since!

Wines & Spirits

DIE OU PASTORIE

SOMERSET WEST

Die Ou Pastorie has, for several years, been one of the Cape's finest restaurants, and the excellent food is complemented by gracious surroundings. The addition a few years ago of spacious en-suite bedroom all with wonderful views, resulted in a splendid guest house offering Victorian style charm in a truly relaxing environment. The personal touc of owners Garry and Karen Roberts is evident throughout the hotel.

Owners *Garry and Karen Roberts.*
16 rooms, swimming pool, Victorian pub.
41 Lourens Street, Somerset West, 7130.
phone *021 852 2120* ***fax*** *021 851 3710*
e-mail *info@dieoupastorie.co.za* ***website*** *www.dieoupastorie.co.za*

ALBOURNE

SOMERSET WEST

Albourne offers comfortable en-suite bedrooms and garden suites, wit private patios. Breakfasts are served on the terrace overlooking the swimming pool and lovely mountain vistas. From this ideal location, o the road to the world renowned Vergelegen Wine Estate, there is a choice of four golf courses. Your hosts will delight with helping with you choice as German, Dutch, French and Spanish are spoken as well as the language of true hospitality. Member of Erinvale Golf Club.

Owners *Trudy and Joop Weterings*
17 rooms, swimming pool,
61 Lourensford Road,Somerset West, 7130.
phone *(021) 852 2184* ***fax*** *(021) 852 7050*
e-mail *info@albourne.co.za* ***website*** *www.albourne.co.za*

CELTIC MANOR

GORDONS BAY

Set in secluded gardens with heated pool this 7-suite Small Luxury Hotel, offers the ultimate in old-fashioned hospitality. Majestic views over Bikini Beach, False Bay and the Harbour are the focal points from the high vantage location above Gordon's Bay on the Sapphire Coast. The A la Carte 'Ocean View Restaurant', health and conference facilities and the 24hr room-service are all under the personal attention of resident owner Jane Thomas.

Owner *Jane Thomas*
7 rooms, swimming pool, sauna, gymnasium, conference facilities.
22 Suikerbossie, Gordons Bay, 7140.
phone *021 856 1313* **toll free** *0800 300030* **fax** *021 856 3862*
e-mail *jane@celticmanor.co.za* **website** *www.celticmanor.sapphirecoast.co.za*

ERINVALE HOTEL ★★★★

SOMERSET WEST

This hotel will charm you with a hospitality for which the Old Cape became world famous. Freshly appointed, exuding luxury, no effort was spared in creating this hotel adjoining the Erinvale Golf Estate. Some rooms under thatch, a sparkling swimming pool, a fine restaurant and an Irish Pub are quality experiences here. A delightful chapel completes the tranquil picture. With historic wine farms as neighbors, quality choices abound.

Manager *Doug Mc Menamin*
57 rooms en-suite, swimming pool, restaurants, bar, conference centre
Lourensford Road, Somerset West 7130. P.O. Box 2941, somerset west 7129
phone *(021) 847 1160* **fax** *(021) 847 1169*
e-mail *hotel@erinvale.co.za* **website** *www.erinvale.co.za*

ARABELLA

Arabella Golf Estate
Length of Course: *6082 metres*
Type of Course: *Parkland*
Holes: *18*
Par: *72*

ARABELLA

Arabella Country Estate
Map reference: 1
Length of Course: 6082 metres
Holes: 18
Type of Course: Parkland
Par: 72
Visitors: Always welcome
Club Professional: Director of Golf- John Bumpsteed 028 284 9383
Tuition: Yes
Club Shop: Yes
Practice Facilities: Warm up area, chipping and putting greens
Hire Facilities: Clubs, trolleys, caddies and drive carts
Catering: Bar, restaurant, halfway house
Location: On the R44 between Kleinmond and Hermanus.
Contact: John Bumpsteed
Postal address: P.O.Box 593 Kleimond 7195
Phone: 028 284 9383
Fax: 028 284 9385
e-mail: maree@w-capehotel.co.za
web: www.arabella.co.za

AN AWARD WINNING ESTATE

The Arabella golf course is at the heart of an award winning estate that encompasses a 'Five Star' hotel, real estate and a protected nature reserve. The awards abound here as every aspect of this development has set standards to compete with any equivalent resort anywhere in the world.

The golf course opened in 1999 and immediately received accolades for the classic design that gently meanders on a natural, undulating landscape bordering the famed Bot Rivier lagoon. On completing its second year of operation, the Golf Digest Magazine's panel of judges deemed the golf course good enough to feature in the top ten golf courses of South Africa. Peter Matkovich, the golf course architect, admits proudly that he was able to achieve a truly well balanced layout, with a mix of long and short par fours, different directional par 3's and a blend of high risk and reward par 5's, all of this on terrain he describes as 'made' for a golf course.

The terrain is indeed quite spectacular, with the land bordering South Africa's largest lagoon and the gentle Kogelberg Mountains as a constant backdrop. Arabella means 'Beautiful Land' in Italian and it is no co-incidence that this translates to the experience to be enjoyed by every golfer on this wonderful golf course.

The whole experience is of expertly manicured Kikuyu fairways that lead to large undulating bent grass greens. The balance is in only two uphill holes and several flat and downhill holes, making this an easy course to walk. The 8th hole, par 5, certainly

7th hole

ranks among one of my most favourite holes, and I am confident that all of you playing this golf course for the first time will judge the four finishing holes as some of the most memorable and challenging you have ever played. This will be especially true if the strong breezes, associated with this area at certain times of the year, are in attendance.

THE COURSE:

2nd Hole - Par 5- 452 metres

This is a seemingly straightforward par 5, which enjoys a wide fairway narrowed slightly by trees on the right and natural fynbos on the left. Bunkers right are visible and come into play for the second shot, while not so noticeable is a large water hazard left of the very large and subtly sloped green.

3rd Hole - Par 4 - 431 metres

This stroke 1 hole is a major challenge and a visually classic one. From the tee water left will lead you to aim right, where two strategically placed bunkers have to be considered. The fairway gently doglegs to the left where a green, sloping steeply uphill from front to back, is bordered by water to its immediate left.

8th hole

On the second nine:
12th Hole - Par 4 - 327 metres

Here the dogleg is to the left and both out of bounds and a severe bunker left of the fairway are immediately noticeable. A wide landing area allows much room on the right, though two bunkers will catch the longer shots. A solitary tree on the left, short of the green, is a consideration, as well as creating some difficulty with regard to perspective. The green sits some distance above the fairway and unseen bunkers right will swallow any shot slightly off target.

13th Hole - Par 5 - 476 metres

A superb par 5 that begins with a large expanse of water fronting the tee and accompanying the fairway for some distance on the right. The fairway is wide and leads gently upwards. Bunkers, both for the tee shot and the second shots, have to be negotiated, while, more sand, cleverly positioned, surrounds a narrow and wide undulating green.

THE ESTATE:

While many 'stay for a while' in the splendid luxury of the hotel, others have decided to invest in a more permanent or semi-permanent lifestyle on the shores of the famed Bot Rivier lagoon. Apart from the golf course and the hotel and spa, the estate comprises 248 housing plots. This translates into only 12% of the entire estate and will explain the lack of interference to both the home-owner and the visiting golfer to their personal environments. This attention to detail, of ensuring a quality experience in a truly natural environment, received world-wide recognition when the development received the prestigious International Standards Award (ISO 14001) for environmental development and management. This monitors several sensitive criteria and this is the first time a golf estate has received this award. The demand for this lifestyle in this remarkable location has been nothing less than spectacular and already several homes (adhering to a stylish and natural architectural theme) are completed. The popularity has been such that currently only re-sales are available!

This care will continue to flourish in the nearby Rooisand Reserve, which will be under the management of the Arabella group in partnership with the Cape Nature Conservation Board. This World Biosphere area will benefit from such professional management and this wonderful destination will no doubt blossom for future generations.

THE WESTERN CAPE HOTEL AND SPA

Though only opened in August 2001, The Western Cape Hotel and Spa has deservedly received recognition as one of the leading hotels in South Africa. This is reflected in the awards that have already been showered on it since opening its luxurious doors. One of these was the Diamond Award by the American Academy of Hospitality Sciences, a renowned body in the hotel industry. The hotel is the first to receive this on the African continent.

The 'first impression' is truly memorable as you enter into the spacious lobby that allows splendid vistas over the golf course, the lagoon and spectacular pool and gardens areas backed by Kogelberg Mountains. These views are made possible as the reception is set on the 5th and top floor of the hotel and many of the amenities and bedrooms are on the floors below. The architecture throughout is a blend of European efficiency and African design with just a hint of Asia. This can be savoured in the spacious and tastefully decorated rooms, where the views on offer can be enjoyed even when lounging in the bath! The facilities include 145 rooms, with a variety of suites, inclusive of two truly aptly named 'Presidential Suites'. On one of my many visits here, I was to witness the arrival of our President, Thabo Mbeki, for an international conference. I am certain that he was impressed by the state of the art conference facilities (able to host 400 delegates and car launches!) and the splendid fare to be enjoyed at one of the two restaurants. The Première restaurant is an A la Carte venue that has enhanced the reputation of Chef Garth Schnier and the Jamani offers a wonderful and varied mix of choices from both a buffet venue and a regular menu. The meeting places in the hotel are Barnabas' bar and the Laguna lounge both, spacious and comfortable. But for the ideal end to either a superb meal or a wonderful memory of a great round of golf, I personally recommend Cristobal's cigar bar.

THE ALTIRASPA:

The success and standards of the facilities and personnel of the AltiraSpa can be measured by the fact that in only the first year of operation, the spa's facilities have had to be increased considerably due to the outstanding demand from both local and overseas guests. The pleasures can begin in the indoor hydro massage pool and be completed around several other pools, including a brine pool, while cascading waterfalls add to a sense of tranquillity. The array of treatments range from massage, beauty therapy, rassoul baths, thalasso therapy and sauna and steam room facilities. Qualified therapists are on hand to introduce yoga, reiki and even, if required, a nutritional, balanced diet for the visitor's stay. The AltiraSpa has already received coveted awards like the Dermalogica Award for quality - and it is to be included in the new edition of 'The top 100 Spa's in the world, published by industry leaders Bernard Burt and Pamela Lechtman. The Western Cape Hotel and Spa Luxury Collection

General Manager *Sebastian Berinato*
117 rooms, 26 suites, 2 Presidential Suites, AltiraSpa, tennis courts,conference centre, golf course.
R44 Kleimond. P.O.Box 593, Kleinmond, 7195.
phone *(028) 284 0000* **fax** *(028) 284 0003*
e-mail *mail@w-capehotel.co.za* **website** *www.arabella.co.za*

Gould's special note:

John Bumpsteed, Director of Golf and Sebastian Berinato, General Manager and Rob Cowling, Director of Wellness, are personal friends of mine and lead a wonderful team.

THE MARINE ★★★★★

HERMANUS

The Marine - Situated on the cliff tops of Hermanus, one of the most beautiful natural landscapes in Africa. The hotel boasts 45 luxury rooms and suites and spectacular views can be captured from your bedroom window, including the Southern Right whales during the months of May to November. Enjoy coastal walks with exquisite views across Walker Bay or while away the day next to the heated swimming pool. A Relais et Châteaux Hotel.

General Manager *Peter Kunz*

45 rooms, helicopter pad, 2 restaurants, heated swimming pool, spa and beauty salon

Marine Drive, Hermanus. P.O. Box 9, Hermanus, 7200.

phone *028 313 1000* ***fax*** *028 313 0160*

e-mail *marine@hermanus.co.za* ***website*** *www.marine-hermanus.co.za*

ARTIST'S HOUSE

HERMANUS

The Artist's House stands in splendid isolation and tranquility, overlooking a large lake in the Hemel-en-Aarde Valley 15 minutes outside of Hermanus. Designed by internationally acclaimed artist and owner Gail Catlin, the rambling house is an ideal retreat for special family weekends, groups of friends or corporate groups needing uninterrupted time. There are ten double rooms decorated in restful natural tones, fabrics and wood, each with a most unusual bathroom.

Owner *Gail Catlin*

6 rooms, 1 self-catering cottage, swimming pool, jacuzzi.

Hemel-en-Aarde Valley, Hermanus. P.O. Box 1242, Sea Point 8060.

phone *021 434 3422* ***fax*** *021 434 7668*

e-mail *shirley@keyside.co.za* ***website*** *www.innside.co.za*

ABALONE LODGE

HERMANUS

Abalone Lodge is an unusually artistic and unique guest lodge located on Siewers Point between the beaches of Hermanus and the town centre. Abalone Lodge's uniquely South African ambience is attested to by the décor which adds to its appeal. All rooms are en-suite with panoramic sea and mountain views which can be enjoyed from private balconies or patios. All you need for a truly memorable experience.

General Manager *Colleen Basson*

7 Rooms, Pool. 306 Main Road Hermanus. P.O. Box 1744, Hermanus, 7200

phone *028 312 3744* **fax** *028 312 4229*

e-mail *res@abalonelodge.co.za* **website** *www.abalonelodge.co.za*

Photo Holler

HERMANUS

Hermanus Golf Course

Length of Course: *5741 metres*

HERMANUS

Hermanus Golf Course

Map reference: *11*

Length of Course: *5741 metres*

Holes: *18*

Type of Course: *Parkland*

Par: *73*

Visitors: *Please book in advance*

Club Professional: *Terry Westbrook 028 312 2271*

Tuition: *Yes*

Club Shop: *Yes*

Practice Facilities: *Driving range, putting green*

Hire Facilities: *Clubs, trolleys, caddies and drive cars*

Catering: *Bar, restaurant, halfway house*

Location: *Main Road, Hermanus*

Contact: *Harry White*

Phone: *028 312 1954*

Fax: *028 312 2333*

e-mail: *harry@hgc.co.za*

web: *www.hgc.co.za*

BABOONS BY THE SEA

Hermanus, on the Cape South Coast, is a charming fishing village famous for the whales that come here annually. Popular with Capetonians as a weekend getaway, its population of 6000 residents swells to over 40 000 during the Christmas and Easter holidays.

Due to this influx, the Hermanus Golf Club experiences heavy traffic at certain times of the year. Despite this, the club, blessed with a dedicated and professional management team, has managed to maintain excellent year round standards. This has been achieved following a well planned maintenance and consistent improvement programme. In recent times, the greens were changed to bent grass to complement the well defined fairways and I believe that this course is truly now a match for any of the other Cape courses.

A resident troop of baboons regularly romps across the fairways of this (almost) by-the-sea golf course. Mountain backdrops and tree-lined fairways provide a pleasant visual experience as you tackle some entertaining golf holes.

The clubhouse has also been upgraded considerably in recent times - while maintaining the quaint and charming look that blends well with the environment. The pro-shop and facilities offered are of a good standard.

The practice range is used regularly by teaching pros for golf clinics, making Hermanus an excellent place in which to improve your golfing skills.

THE COURSE

5th Hole - Par 4 - 281 metres

The baboons can usually be found around the 5th and 6th holes, so let's start at the 5th, a hole that doglegs to the left and is lined with trees to prevent you from taking a direct route. There is plenty of fairway to find on the right and anything hit there will leave you needing a mid or short iron to reach the green slightly above you. A bunker on the front left and a sharp slope to the right stand guard over this green.

6th Hole - Par 4 - 394 metres

This demanding par 4 has a water hazard all the way along the right hand side and trees to the left of the fairway. A mound encroaching onto the fairway provides a good target and your tee shot should be to the right. The long second is to a green that slopes uphill from front to back and anything pushed right of the green will find the water hazard looming close by.

7th Hole - Par 3 - 172 metres

It always requires a really good shot to reach this long par 3. A bunker on the left and one on the right need to be avoided and you will find some tricky little slopes on either side, or at the back, before you return to the green, should you have missed it.

THE AREA

If you have time to spare, there are spectacular views of the town from Rotary Drive on the road from Cape Town. From this vantage point you will also be able to see the unspoilt stretch of Grotto Beach with the lagoon behind it.

The Old Harbour museum is worth a visit and the new harbour area will find many a fisherman trying his luck from the dockside. Hermanus has another unique selling point, the Southern Right Whales come here to calve and between March and October, it is usually possible to watch these mysterious yet marvellous creatures from the cliffs above the sea.

MULLIGANS GUEST LODGE

HERMANUS

Situated right on the fairways of the Hermanus Golf Club, with direct acces to the Clubhouse, this delightful and hospitable guest house provides an ideal location for all the attractions of the area. There are spacious en-suit double bedrooms, all with DSTV and M-Net and under-floor heating. Ther is a pool and braai area and a hospitality bar. The attention of your hosts and the sensational breakfasts are memorable moments.

Owners *Yvonne and Paul Jansen*

5 rooms - all with telephones , swimming pool, braai area, secure parking.

275 Main Road, Hermanus, 7200.

phone *028 312 4469* ***fax*** *028 313 1293*

e-mail *mullig@mweb.co.za* ***website*** *www.hermanus.co.za/accom/mulligans*

WHALE ROCK LODGE ★★★★

HERMANUS

Situated near the new harbour in Hermanus, this beautiful thatched lodge offers sumptuous accommodation in a secluded garden setting, and the hospitality here is almost tangible. Each individual and delightfull decorated room is en-suite with its own sitting area. A full breakfast is served in the lodge's own poolside restaurant. There is secure parking Gould's special note: This is always one of my favourite stops as I write this guide.

Owner *Shelagh Milton*

11 rooms, swimming pool, secure parking.

26 Springfield Avenue, West Cliff, Hermanus, 7200.

phone *028 313 0014* ***fax*** *028 312 2932*

e-mail *wrl@hermanus.co.za* ***website*** *www.whalerock.co.za*

19th HOLE GUEST LODGE ★★★

HERMANUS

The name of this delightful lodge tells you its situation overlooking the golf course. What it does not tell you is the personal attention you will receive from hosts Brian and Sandy. Brian is a fisherman, and will delight in taking you shark or whale watching while Sandy will cook the legendary breakfasts the lodge is known for. All this while you enjoy the comfortable en-suite rooms with golf course and mountain views.

Owners *Brian and Sandy McFarlane*
5 Rooms, Secure parking
281 Main Road, Hermanus. P.O. Box 191, Hermanus, 7200
phone *028 312 2766* **fax** *028 312 2766*
e-mail *19thhole@netactive.co.za* **website** *www.hermanus.co.za/accom/19th_hole*

WHALE COTTAGE HERMANUS ★★★★

HERMANUS

Whale Cottage Hermanus, sister guest house to Whale Cottage Camps Bay and Whale Cottage Bakoven, is a stately double storey house offering the best whale watching and unobstructed seaviews guests could wish for. The cliff paths in Hermanus, from which the Southern Right whales and their calves can be seen, are just 100 meters from the guest house, across the road. Wir sprechen Deutsch.

Owner *Christiane von Ulmenstein*
5 Rooms, Swimming pool. Whale Cottage loyalty card.
P.O.Box 200, HERMANUS 7200. 38 Westcliff Drive, Hermanus.
phone *028 313-0929* **fax** *028 313-0912*
e-mail *hermanus@whalecottage.com* **website** *www.whalecottage.com*

Mossel Bay Golf Estate

Length of Course: *5763 metres*

MOSSEL BAY

Mossel Bay Golf Estate — **Map reference:** 18
Length of Course: 5763 metres — **Holes:** 18
Type of Course: Links — **Par:** 72
Visitors: No restrictions
Club Professional: None — 044 690 8305
Tuition: No — **Club Shop:** Yes
Practice Facilities: Putting green, chipping area
Hire Facilities: Caddies
Catering: Bar, halfway house
Location: 17th Avenue, Mossel Bay
Contact: Jannie Lourens
Postal address: P.O.Box 199, Mossel Bay, 6500
Phone: 044 691 2379 — **Fax:** 044 691 3819
e-mail: mosselbaygolfclub@freemail.absa.co.za

SEE THE SEA FROM EVERY TEE

The Mossel Bay golf course is hilly and the advantage of this undulating terrain is that views of the sea are visible from every hole. These views are also now available to several permanent residents who have bought properties made available by an innovative development surrounding this golf course 'where you can see the sea from every tee.'

The success of the property development has had a marked effect on the golf course. The golf course, always regarded as an enjoyable country experience, has been substantially upgraded to include some re-design, the introduction of new holes, a reticulation system and the complete upgrade of its greens. You can still see the sea from every tee, but the experience now includes sweeping manicured fairways leading to large and challenging greens. These greens, designed by Danie Obermeyer of Danie Obermeyer Golf Design, who was retained to upgrade the whole course, are sometimes severe, sometimes subtle and always memorable.

The golf course has now gained a reputation among local and overseas visitors as a 'must play' venue when visiting this part of the famed Garden Route area.

Although the course is near the sea, it cannot be classified as a true links course even though this is the feeling you will get here. Low bush lines the fairways and you will encounter sandy lies and heather-like bush that wraps around your club with great enthusiasm!

Several of the tees are from high vantage points leading to fairways well below, while the undulating and hilly terrain leads some holes back up to greens well above the landing areas of the holes. Local wind conditions are likely to make the degree of difficulty variable depending on the strength of the prevailing breezes.

The clubhouse has been completely renovated and now complements the standards set on the course, to offer a wonderful off-course experience at this friendly and welcoming club. An additional asset has been the introduction of a substantial practice range.

6th hole

THE COURSE

While some holes have been altered from the original design, the resulting improvements to this course have only served to fine-tune this enjoyable golf course. The Mossel Bay 'feel' has not been lost and the sparkling blue of the Indian Ocean backing nature's green valleys, that are so much a part of this undulating landscape, will be forever memorable.

The greens can be ferociously quick at times, but they are in excellent condition and you will find yourself enjoying the putting surfaces no matter what speed they are on your day of play.

3rd hole - Par 4 - 388 metres

This is a memorable par 4. It is a long hole and with its nearly 400 meter distance, into the wind, only the long hitters can reach it in two. From the elevated tee, the fairway runs downhill all the way to the green that is backed by the beauty of the ocean. The fairway is seemingly wide and trouble free, but strategically placed bunkers and rough provide some brakes to a smooth ride to this visually delightful hole.

17th hole - Par 5 - 482 metres

This is a par 5, length 493m from the back tee . When the wind is from behind it seems quite easy. It is tempting to go for the green for your second shot but four bunkers are waiting for you. Again, the Indian Ocean backdrop makes for a splendid picture. As mentioned, downwind this downhill hole has a gentle feel. However, beware, it is a very different story when the wind is blowing against you. It becomes impossible to reach the green in 2. Even the bravest of the long hitters will find bunkers waiting for them. This stroke 2 hole with all its beauty, will certainly put you to the test.

11th hole

THE ESTATE

Urs Winholz, of Innside Investments, whose vision it was to implement a housing development around the scenic environments of the Mossel Bay golf course, acknowledges that the success of his development has been that the 'climate was right'. I would add that there were several ingredients that augmented this success.

Indeed the climate is one of those ingredients, as Mossel Bay is famous for its year-round temperate climate. Mother Nature provided natural undulations and magnificent views as well as craggy hillsides, crashing waves and an array of colourful and indigenous flora to complete the picture. The other ingredients were the quality of building, complemented by the value-for-money aspect of buying into this secure and special location.

That it is special will be understood when the visitor notes the views available to the permanent homeowner. This is further emphasized when realising that there is a private and protected nature reserve as a back garden. Wonderful flora hangs on craggy cliff-sides, while the unspoilt scenic landscape lends itself to gentle soulful walks and truly tranquil moments.

11th green

THE AREA

Mossel Bay was named in 1601 by the Dutch navigator; Paulus van Caerden, some one hundred years after the Portuguese navigators used it as a fresh-water supply station. An abundance of mussels lining the shores gave rise to the name. The wonderful, temperate climate and position overlooking the sheltered bay and beaches attract tens of thousands of holidaymakers annually. Water sports feature high on the list of activities here. Mossel Bay has one of the highest numbers of sunshine hours of any coastal town in the world, which indicates the sort of conditions that you can expect here.
If the era of the early navigators fascinates you, then you will love the Maritime museum, with its full-scale replica of Bartholomew Diaz' caravelle, the sailing ship that first rounded the tip of Africa and opened the way to trade in India and beyond.

MUNRO MANOR

MOSSEL BAY

The view from the terrace of this excellent Garden Route guest house will forever prove memorable. You will overlook Madeba beach, the Indian Ocean and the Outeniqua Mountains in the distance. A personal touch comes from Marika Thomatos, who has single-handedly created 10 en-suite rooms, alive with bright and quality fabrics, enhanced by clever blending of artefacts and paintings throughout the rooms. There is also a swimming pool with a bar and 'braai' facility.

Owner *Marika Thomatos*

10 Rooms, Swimming pool. 8 George Street, Mossel Bay. PO Box 72, Mossel Bay 6500.

phone *044 691 3440* **fax** *044 691 1146*

e-mail *munromanor@mweb.co.za* **website** *www.munromanor.co.za*

OLD POST OFFICE TREE MANOR★★★/★★★★

MOSSEL BAY

*The Old Post Office Tree Manor Hotel is located adjacent to the renowned 'Old Post Office Tree' monument. This historic seaside hotel offers travellers a choice of either *** en-suite rooms or ****self catering suites. The complex is set in a prime location overlooking the sweeping bay, whilst being central to the beach, harbour and center of town. The hotel is home to the famous Café Gannet sea food restaurant and you can expect true country hospitality with helpful and friendly service from all the staff.*

General Manager *Emma Booysen*

22 rooms, 8 suites, swimming pool, blue oyster bar, secure parking.

Church Street, Mossel Bay. P.O. Box 349, Mossel Bay 6500

phone *044 691 3738* **fax** *044 691 3104*

e-mail *book@oldposttree.co.za* **website** *www.oldposttree.co.za*

THE POINT ★★★

MOSSEL BAY

Superbly positioned on the rocks at Mossel Bay's famous lighthouse, 50 sea-facing en-suite rooms with private balconies overlooking the Indian Ocean. A huge tidal pool right in front of the hotel offers safe bathing, whilst surfers can enjoy one of the best surfing venues on the coast line. A 15 km walking trail along the coast starts at the hotel. The Lighthouse Restaurant and bar cater for all tastes and appetites

Owner *Louis Harris*
50 Rooms, Tidal pool, Conference facilities
The Point, Point Road, Mossel Bay. P.O.Box 449, Mossel Bay 6500
phone *044 691 3512* ***fax*** *044 691 3513*
e-mail *thepoint@pointhotel.co.za* ***website*** *www.pointhotel.co.za*

DOLPHIN BAY HOTEL

MOSSEL BAY

Overlooking the shimmering blue bay of Mossel Bay, with the Outeniqua Mountains in the distance, the new Dolphin Bay Hotel offers 109 exceptionally spacious bedrooms with the best views in the bay. All have a private bath/shower, balcony, telephone, DSTV and coffee/tea facilities. Comfortable conference facilities currently accommodate up to 45 delegates (soon to be extended). Internationally experienced hoteliers & conference organisers will ensure that your holiday or business stay is a successful and memorable one.

General Manager *Heinz Hoffgen-Berger*
109 rooms, conference centre, swimming pool, ample parking.
Louis Fourie Road, Mossel Bay. P.O.Box 225, Mossel Bay, 6500
phone *044 691 9001* ***fax*** *(044) 691 3435*
e-mail *info@dolphinbay.co.za* ***website*** *www.dolphinbay.co.za*

FANCOURT

Home of The Presidents Cup 2003

FANCOURT

Fancourt Hotel and Country Club Estate

Map reference: *8*

Courses: *Four 18 holes. The Montagu, The Outeniqua, The Links, Bramble Hill*

Visitors: *Private Resort - open to guests staying in the hotel. Bramble Hill is a public course open to all.*

Club Professional: *Director of Golf Fancourt: Wayne Krambeck*
Director of Golf Links: Mark Wiltshire

Practice facilities: *Golf Academy, warm up area, chipping and putting greens*

Hire Facilities: *Clubs, carts, caddies and drive carts*

Catering: *There are 3 Clubhouses - all with full catering and bar facilities.*

Location: *Montagu Street, Blanco, George.*

Contact: *Tertia Kruger*

Postal address: *P.O.Box 2266, Blanco, George 6530*

Phone: *044 804 0000* ***Fax:*** *044 804 0700*

e-mail: *hotel@fancourt.co.za* ***web:*** *www.fancourt.com*

SETTING FOR A PRESIDENT

In November 2003, Fancourt will host The Presidents Cup. This international challenge between the top golfers from the USA and the best of the Rest of the World (excluding the European Ryder Cup countries) will be watched by a television audience of an estimated 400 million viewers. The competition is under the chairmanship of our President Thabo Mbeki.

Our president is confident that there can be no better venue to showcase the wonder of golf in South Africa, the beauty of the country and the remarkable world class facilities to be enjoyed in this spectacular part of our country, known as the Garden Route.

The Presidents Cup will be played on 'The Links', one of Fancourt's four 18 hole courses. 'The Links' was commissioned by Dr Hasso Plattner, the visionary owner of the Fancourt development. Over the past three years, Gary Player, in conjunction with his famed golf course architect, Phil Jacobs, has been crafting this 'piece de resistance' where the international golfing gladiators will test their skills. Built on a former aerodrome, 700 000 cubic tons of earth were moved, 10 hectares of wetlands introduced and high grassy mounds were covered with hand planted grasses. Jack Nicklaus,

17th hole - Montagu

who is the non-playing captain of the USA Presidents Cup team, is quoted as saying that this is the best inland links he has encountered on his travels. "It is rare to have so much land and space in which to introduce the facets of a traditional links layout. The mounds, fairway grasses and the variety of green sizes have all moulded this into a replica of those old traditional links courses," Nicklaus concluded.
Gary Player, who is the Captain of the International team, will, of course, have home (and designer) advantage. This will also apply to Ernie Els, South Africa's number one player, as the 'Big Easy' spends much of his time at Fancourt when he is 'home' from his many travels.
'The Links' apart, Fancourt has three other splendid courses.

THE COURSES

Here I declare my undeniable enjoyment of these courses, as I was involved since the beginning of Fancourt, both as the Promotional Manager and subsequently General Manager. So I list my own personal feature holes for each course.
***The Montagu**: voted number one golf course in South Africa in 2000 by the Golf Digest panel of judges, it remains at the top of the tree in South Africa. Recent bunker improvements and the lengthening of holes are the new challenges to a course famed for its scenic beauty and exceptional manicuring.*

4th hole - Montagu

2nd Hole - Par 3 - 166 metres

Well, I had a hole in one here! Several tee choices can make this a short or long par 3. Whichever tee is in play, the visual impact is memorable. The target sits pictorially well below the launching pads. There is a creek that runs along the right and three, hardly noticeable, pot bunkers to the left. The green slopes sharply upwards from front to back and leads to a well shaped bunker at the back.

The Outeniqua *- This course has also had recent changes to its bunkers and this visually delightful challenge enjoys the added bonus of an abundance of trees being introduced over several years. Memorable water features are in play on many of the holes and the garden surrounds of many of the tees and greens are a constant blaze of colour.*

3rd hole - Outeniqua

17th Hole - Par 5 - 462 metres

A downhill par 5- suites my game! Fairway bunkers are to be avoided off the tee. While the longer hitters can reach this in two, the degree of difficulty has increased in recent times due to a water feature left of the green being extended to front two thirds of this target. There is a narrow entrance between the water and a bunker right. Most players, whether looking to get on in two, or more prudently with three shots, will require an accurate shot to this large, flat green.

Bramble Hill *- This is the newest of Fancourt's four courses. It is set on undulating, indeed some times hilly, terrain. The sloping fairways require you to have an array of shots in your repertoire. Several clever, strategically placed, water hazards will prove testing and scenically memorable.*

3rd and 4th hole - Bramble

3rd hole - Par 4 - 365 metres

The tee shot has to contend with water all along the left side of the fairway finishing in front of the green. Having put your ball in play, your approach shot is over water with a view of high, sloping dunes backed by the Outeniqua Mountains. There is plenty of room right but the wider you go the longer the shot over the water.

16th hole - The Links

The Links -*Just the thought of the impending challenge between Tiger Woods and Ernie Els here will focus the attention. This is a walking course and the sandy paths that lead from tee to fairway and from green to tee lead through grassy mounds and tranquil water landscapes. Unlike its genuine predecessors, the famous links of Scotland and Ireland, this is an inland golf course. However, I assure you, there is an aura here that will have you convinced you can hear the sea lapping on the shores!*

15th hole - Par 5 - 461 metres

15th hole - The Links

Every hole on the links has its own individual name. This one is called 'Roon the Bend'. The fairway sweeps in a long dogleg left hugging the water of the wetlands all the way to the green. The task off the tee is to choose how much of the water to take on to reach the undulating and rolling fairway. The next challenge is to find the green and avoid its sand and water guardians.

Gould's special note:

The magic of all four courses is that they are nestled below the scenic Outeniqua Mountains. These provide a constant backdrop and add to the beauty created below them. Outeniqua is the 'San' word meaning 'Land of Honey'-I cannot think of a better description!

THE ESTATE

Dr Hasso and Sabine Plattner, originally from Germany, bought Fancourt just prior to our first democratic elections in 1994. Their vision and enthusiasm for this country and for Fancourt in particular, is reflected in the success of this remarkable world-class resort. Thatched style homes and Cape Colonial houses now line the expanses of the fairways and the water and manicured gardens of this 515 hectare estate. It is a testament to the planners, the architects and the management team at Fancourt, that these stylish homes blend naturally into this scenic landscape, while allowing privacy for both the resident and the golfer. The quality continues in the range of amenities available for both the visitor and the resident. There are tennis courts, a leisure centre with cinema, indoor heated family pool, an outdoor pool and a delicatessen, as well as biking and walking trails. A fully fledged golf academy, with covered bays, offers the developing golfer professional tuition, while the more accomplished player can warm up either at the academy or at the separate warm up facility.

THE HOTEL

At the heart of the estate is the original Manor House. This original homestead, built by Sir Henry Fancourt White, now houses 30 of the rooms of the 100 bedrooms. The remaining rooms are in Garden Suites overlooking dams, beautiful gardens or the Montagu golf course. The hotel encompasses several splendid restaurants, the main clubhouse housing the pro-shop, visitors and members bar and the health and beauty spa. This healthy environment is complemented by a spectacular indoor pool area, known as the Roman Baths.

Resort General Manager *Ingrid Diesel*
100 Rooms and privately owned lodges
Swimming pools, tennis, bowls, hiking and biking trails.
Montagu Street, Blanco, George 6530
phone *(044) 804 0000* ***fax*** *(044) 804 0700*
e-mail *hotel@fancourt.co.ca* ***website*** *www.fancourt.com.*

Gould's Special note:

The Presidents Cup, due to be played in November 2003, is run under the auspices of the USPGA. Dennis Alpert is the Chief Executive Officer of The Presidents Cup and has been in South Africa for over a year in preparation for this spectacular event. He has developed a passion for this country and Fancourt in particular. I am pleased to quote him. "Fancourt is truly a world class facility. We have never before had such an amazing venue."

FANCOURT

GEORGE

George Golf Course | ***Map reference:*** *9*
Length of Course: *5777 metres* | ***Holes:*** *18*
Type of Course: *Parkland* | ***Par:*** *72*
Visitors: *Booking recommended*
Club Professional: *Vaughn Tucker 044 873 4254*
Tuition: *Yes* | ***Club Shop:*** *Yes*
Practice Facilities: *Putting greens*
Hire Facilities: *Clubs, trolleys, caddies and drive carts*
Catering: *Bar, halfway house*
Location: *C.J. Langehoven Street, George*
Contact: *Human Weideman*
Postal address: *P.O.Box 81, George 6530*
Phone: *044 873 6116* | ***Fax:*** *044 874 6191*
e-mail: *george@netactive* | ***web:*** *www.georgegolfclub.co.za*

CHARMING AND WONDERFUL

In recent years, a central dam was introduced to this classic layout. This has added visual splendour to the layout, which remains one of the most popular stops for golfers, year after year. The course follows undulating terrain through a variety of tree species, and manages to convey the sense of a pleasant outing in a well planned garden.

The Garden Route is one of South Africa's major tourist attractions and it is because of this that the George golf course enjoys year round patronage. Although George has a reputation for cold, wet winters (hence the car registration for the area being CAW named by the locals as Cold and Wet!) you might find yourself experiencing four seasons in one day, as the weather patterns here are unpredictable. Please do not be put off by this. It is unpredictable, but for months of the year it is a pleasure to enjoy the temperate climate unique to this area. A climate such as this lends itself to green lush fairways, green foliage and the maintenance of greens. The introduction of bent grass greens, several years ago, has lifted the reputation of this already highly regarded golf venue. The putting surfaces are immaculate year round and they are large with subtle slopes, allowing for a variety of pin placements. The whole course is well guarded by trees and the fairways and greens protected by several well shaped bunkers. In a recent survey by a panel of experts from the Golf Digest Magazine, George golf course deservedly was voted in the top ten layouts of South Africa. This prompted a local scribe to point out that the car registration CAW now stands for Charming and Wonderful!

THE COURSE

7th Hole - Par 4 - 411 metres

This is a genuinely tough stroke 1 hole. With the Outeniqua Mountain range as a backdrop, you will be hitting to an uphill fairway lined with trees. As you aim for the tall pines in the distance, you will note that the curve of this hole must be to the right. As you reach the crest of the fairway for the second shot, the fairway runs sharply downhill and back up to a plateau green. A steep bank left will run your ball into a forest. Stay right and the natural contours will help the ball back towards the target.

18th Hole - Par 4 - 388 metres

This excellent finishing hole has the fairway sloping from right to left. You will need to aim right to allow the ball to head back towards the centre. The trouble is on the left, where thick bush and the dam line the fairway. The fairway narrows in its approach to the elevated green with a thicket on the right catching the fade. On reaching the green, encircling banks will bring the ball back to this large, two-tier green guarded by a bunker on each side.

THE AREA

The mountains offer hiking trails and wondrous views. It is worth driving up the pass (possibly with a picnic) to savour the scenery. Victoria Bay, Wilderness, Glentana and Herold's Bay all have distinctive beaches. Just outside George, past the long stretch of Wilderness Beach, is the lake district of South Africa. Here, large expanses of water house abundant bird life and diverse water sports are on offer. A delightful way to savour this fascinating coast is to travel from George to Knysna by the unique vintage steam train. This winds its way along coastal cliffs, across beaches, lakes and through forests to the rhythm of the hissing, puffing and panting of the proud iron horse, known as 'The Outeniqua Choo Tjoe'.

PROTEA WILDERNESS ★★★

WILDERNESS

The Protea Hotel Wilderness Resort is situated in the heart of the Garden Route and offers easy access to all golf courses and tourist sites in the area. The resort also offers a range of sporting and leisure activities, such as swimming pools, tennis, squash and an in-house spa. Bedrooms are stylish and comfortably appointed, offering views and garden settings. Socialize in the cozy Outeniqua Bar or enjoy the scenic views from the terrace.

General Manager *Neil Stanley Dorsett*
155 rooms, swimming pools, conference facilities, spa, tennis, squash
George Road, Wilderness. P.O. Box 6, Wilderness, 6560
phone *044 877 1110* ***fax*** *044 877 0600*
e-mail *reservations@proteawilderness.co.za* ***website*** *www.proteahotels.com/wildernessresort*

PROTEA HOTEL KING GEORGE ★★★

GEORGE

This premier hotel has a unique location on the 11th fairway of the George golf course. The rooms are spacious, with 2 double beds and all are en-suite with bath and showers, as well as satellite television. Lovers of good food will enjoy the Fairway Terrace Restaurant, or indulge in the warm atmosphere of the Rex Tavern.

General Manager *John Creighton*
64 rooms, 2 swimming pools, tennis, conference facilities.
King George Drive, King George Park.
P.O. Box 9292, George, 6530.
phone *044 874 7659* ***fax*** *044 874 7664*
e-mail *king.george@pixie.co.za* ***website*** *www.proteahotels.com/kinggeorge*

GOLF EDITION PICTURES
"SIGNIFICANT MOMENTS"
from Dieter Olaf Klama
Here are 3 of his 8 famous golf edition pictures:

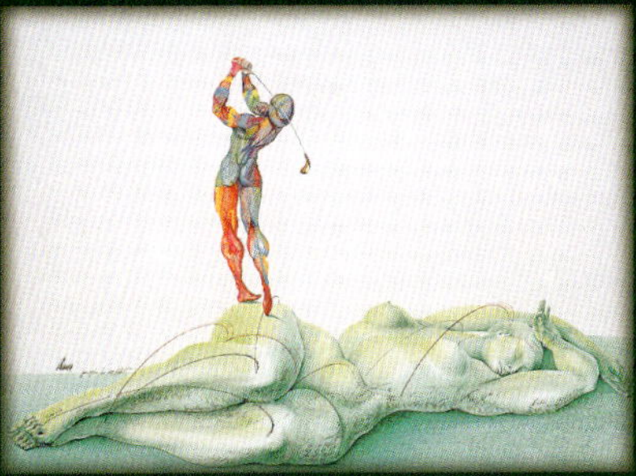

AUGUSTE 970cm x 680 cm

DIETER OLAF KLAMA

Is among Europe's most successful cartoonists. His pictures of automobiles, sports and the world of the computer have been hung in numerous European galleries. Many of his works have been awarded prizes all over the world.

T-OFF 970cm x 680 cm

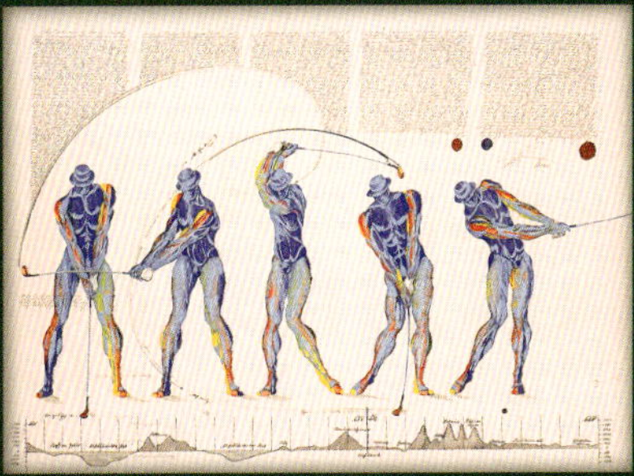

PERFECT LESSON 970cm x 680 cm

"The harmony of a Swing can create a work of art" philosophized Jack Niklaus, the American golf legend, **"It is the spirit that makes the ball fly"**, he said when he saw Klama's golf edition.

ONLY A LIMITED EDITION - HAND SIGNED BY THE ARTIST
bay print, Cape Town Phone: +27 21 553 4330
or E-mail: bayprwuest@iafrica.com

OAKHURST MANOR★★★

GEORGE

This delightful thatch-roofed hotel with dazzling white gables is set in the heart of George. From the open-plan reception, encompassing the cosy bar, restaurant and lounge with its warm fireplace, you will feel at home. Glowing yellowwood and rich terracotta floors is a feature, while the en-suite rooms create a feel of classic country style. Modern facilities such as shower, bath, television, radio and telephone are in all the rooms.

General Manager *Judy Ritchie*
25 rooms
Corner of Meade and Cathedral Street. P.O. Box 9416, George, 6530.
phone *044 874 7130* **fax** *044 874 7131*
e-mail *info@oakhursthotel.co.za* **website** *www.oakhursthotel.co.za*

FAR HILLS COUNTRY HOTEL★★★

GEORGE

Far Hills Country Hotel, situated in magnificent landscaped gardens, has a selection of function & conference rooms, well appointed with antique furnishings and original artwork. The luxurious bedrooms, all have spectacular views from their own private balcony, while the Deluxe Rooms feature cosy fireplaces and private bars. The a-la carte restaurant has an adjoining cellar stocked with a selection of fine Cape wines. Alternatively, experience the Japanese Cuisine in the intimate Sushi & Teppanyaki Bar.

General Manager *Beverley Robinson*
50 rooms, swimming pool, conference facilities.
N2 Road between George and Wilderness. P.O.Box 10, George, 6530.
phone *044 889 0000* **fax** *044 889 0001*
e-mail *farhills@mweb.co.za* **website** *www.farhillscountryhotel.fsnet.co.uk*

Oudtshoorn Golf Course ***Map reference:*** *20*
Length of Course: *6210 metres* ***Holes:*** *18*
Type of Course: *Parkland* ***Par:*** *72*
Visitors: *No restrictions*
Club Professional: *None*
Tuition: *None* ***Club Shop:*** *Yes*
Practice Facilities: *Putting green*
Hire Facilities: *Clubs, trollies, caddies and drive carts*
Catering: *Bar, halfway house*
Location: *Saint Saviour Street, Oudtshoorn*
General Manager: *David Duncan*
Postal address: *P.O.Box 331, Oudtshoorn 6620*
Phone: *044 272-4201* ***Fax:*** *044 279-2609*

WELL PEPPERED

Ostriches thrive in the year round hot and dry areas and since Oudtshoorn is renowned for its ostrich farms, you should have some indication of the type of weather to expect. You could be forgiven for anticipating a golf course with dry brown fairways and sandy brown greens, but the golf course at Oudtshoorn will surprise you! There is little doubt that the low rainfall of this area has made it a challenge to the golf committee, which has somehow succeeded in introducing a reticulation system that has managed to defy the natural environment.

In recent years, ongoing improvements to the course are resulting in a year-round quality that has transformed this country course into a worthwhile stop for the travelling golfer. The best time to play this golf course, nevertheless, remains in winter, especially if the Southern Cape coastal courses are being pounded with rain. You will enjoy playing along the green fairways lined with an abundance of pepper trees, tall palms, water (yes there is some!), Karoo-style scrubland and thick blue gums, all of which will ensure that your golfing skills are tested.

The rough is rough and sometimes rocky and the greens may surprise you with their consistency. The clubhouse is small, but the bar itself is large and always welcoming.

Gould's special note:

This is a social club that has embraced the importance of the visiting golfer and you may find yourself enticed to join in at the 19th hole with some of the lively ostrich farmers of the area.

THE COURSE

11th Hole - Par 4 - 342 metres

A tall, thin pine stands sentry at the tee on this narrow, yet attractive, hole. The elevated green can be seen clearly in the distance and the only concern is for accuracy off the tee. It is prudent to favour the left as, after the initial infringement of trees, the fairway opens up on that side. As you walk up you will notice that the fairway is fairly wide, narrowing uphill as it approaches the green, guarded by a bunker front left. Should your shot be slightly too long, a solitary mound behind the green is of concern.

12th Hole - Par 3 - 155 metres

The dam fronting this tee, with its resident bird life, is worth a moment away from golf. As the green is some distance from the water, the extra gravity over water should for once not pose a problem. Your target is to a long, two-tiered green with a gentle mound to the right and a small bank on the back left. The test of this short hole is to read the speed and slope of the green.

13th Hole - Par 5 - 497 metres

For me, this hole encompasses the real 'feel' of the Oudtshoorn golf course. All around the hillside slopes is Klein Karoo scrubland, with your target a trio of pepper trees at the curve of this dogleg right. Should you hit to the right of these, you will thread your second shot through a gap created by more trees on the right. For the long hitters, a fairway bunker right and well short of the green might create a problem. A small bunker left in the rough will catch a pulled shot. The green slopes from left to right and has a deceptive incline from front to back.

THE AREA

Anyone who has visited a Japanese nightclub and has been surprised to see ostrich feathers in use may be even more surprised to learn that these ostrich plumes were exported to Japan from Oudtshoorn. Although the heyday of the Ostrich Barons, who built vast mansions that still stand as monuments to great, but short-lived riches, is over, the farms still export a considerable quantity of feathers. The main function of the farms today however, is as tourist attractions, and they are well worth a visit. Apart from seeing these strange creatures (that by the way do not bury their heads in the sand) you may be fascinated by the product range that this lanky, gawky bird provides. The Cango caves, the cheetah and the crocodile parks are also of interest in this area.

LA PLUME ★★★★

OUDTSHOORN

La Plume Guesthouse is a Victorian styled homestead dating back to 1902. Situated in the tranquil surroundings of a working ostrich farm, alfalfa and vine farm, amidst the scenic Elephants River Valley with spectacular views of the Swartberg Mountain range. The owners, Barte and Karin du Toit, third generation on the farm, consistently stride toward perfection in combining the best of two worlds, top class luxurious accommodation and delectable cuisine.

***Owners** Bartel and Karin du Toit*
9 rooms, swimming pool
On the R62 to Calitzdorp, follow signs to La Plume.
P.O. Box 1202, Oudtshoorn, 6620
***phone** 044 272 7516* ***fax** 044 272 3892*
***e-mail** laplume@mweb.co.za* ***website** www.laplume.co.za*

KNYSNA

Knysna Golf Course
Length of Course: *5831 metres*
Type of Course: *Parkland*
Holes: *18*
Par: *73*

KNYSNA

Knysna Golf Course — ***Map reference:*** *13*
Length of Course: *5831 metres* — ***Holes:*** *18*
Type of Course: *Parkland* — ***Par:*** *73*
Visitors: *Any day, but should make prior arrangements with pro*
Club Professional: *Louis Esselen*
Tuition: *Yes* — ***Club Shop:*** *Yes*
Practice Facilities: *Yes – own balls, putting green*
Hire Facilities: *Clubs, trolleys, caddies and drive carts (bookings essential)*
Catering: *Bar, halfway house*
Location: *Howard Street, Hunters Home*
Contact: *Quinten Webster*
Postal address: *P.O.Box 110 , Knysna 6570*
Phone: *044 384 1150 - Simon* — ***Fax:*** *044 384 1150 / (044) 384 1033*
e-mail: *golfclub@mweb.co.za* — ***web:*** *www.knysnagolf.co.za*

BLUE LAGOON

Knysna is one of South Africa's favourite and most scenic resort areas. With its spectacular lagoon, surrounding hills, forests and river, there is plenty on offer for the holiday visitor. Knysna's flat golf course, threading its way through tall blue gums and pines, has always had much to recommend it. An upgrade programme, introduced in 1998, has continued over the intervening years, and the course has undergone some considerable alteration, resulting in an even better golfing experience.

New water features have been introduced and real attention paid to the bunkering throughout the layout. The major task was to improve the existing greens. That this has been successfully implemented can be seen from the clubhouse for the eighteenth hole now has a superb bent grass surface covering a large undulating area. Shapely and well manicured bunkers protecting the green add to what is now a substantial finishing challenge.

The course nevertheless remains where you will enjoy a gentle stroll through tree-lined fairways and not experience the fatigue you might on the more testing courses. The surrounding hills provide scenic backdrops and there is a great variety of trees, flowers and bird-life to watch out for. The quaint clubhouse has a pleasant halfway house with a terrace and welcoming bar. The atmosphere is friendly and relaxing, so enjoy!

THE COURSE

8th Hole - Par 3 - 152 metres

As you stand on the tee, this tricky, short hole appears to be a straightforward par 3. The green is framed by two small trees on the fairway and pampas grass provides a scenic backdrop. However, there is water fronting the green. This becomes obvious only by the sleepers that front the target and make for a scenic, if challenging, moment. The green, not completely visible from the tee, is one of the new, large, bent grass greens introduced throughout the course and the bail out shot will be to take more club than usual. Beware - as more water backs this green.

9th Hole - Par 5 - 442 metres

A narrow tee provides the launching pad to this par 5. From here you will see a wide fairway, though your mental perspective might narrow this as trouble lies on both sides. Pampas grass and reeds escort you all the way to the green and a variety of trees add to the visual effect. As mentioned, the fairway is wide and, staying straight, you will reach a green that doglegs left around a deep and large bunker fronting it.

On the second nine, the 16th is special
16th Hole - Par 5 - 502 metres

On the left side of the fairway, blue gums and pines guide the fairway gently to the right. A similar assortment of trees guards the right. The mountain silhouette and residential houses sprinkled along the slopes give you the 'Knysna feel' of tranquillity. The fairway is wide but narrows towards the green, where water provides a testing moment to an elevated target with a long and narrow sand trap guarding the right.

THE AREA

The Knysna lagoon is the heart of this area which is blessed with forests, rivers, beautiful beaches and even an unusual nature reserve. The Featherbed Nature Reserve situated on one of the Knysna Heads, leading out to sea, was established by William Smith, who was responsible for discovering the Coelacanth, a nasty looking fish, but one of great historical interest. I always enjoy a day trip to the reserve and recommend that you look for the Resident Cranes (South Africa's national bird).

The town itself has a craft market feel and is famous for its wood shops, good restaurants and artistic flair.

Good beaches can be found at Brenton-on-Sea and, if you should head that way, stop in at Belvidere for a good view of the lagoon. For the oyster lover, a visit to the oyster factory is a must and it may be an idea to top this off with a visit to the Waterfront development which offers a of choice of restaurants and shopping.

Gould's special note:

Thiesen Island, in the middle of the lagoon, is in the process of being transformed from housing a former timber mill, to housing permanent residents. The unique style of the homes and carefully planned environmental aspects of this ambitious project have considerably impressed me on my regular visits there.

KNYSNA

This log chalet resort, on prime lagoon-front property, is within easy walking distance of the charming town of Knysna. There are 35 architecturally designed, fully serviced and equipped, authentic log chalets, with either self-catering or bed and breakfast options. The origina manor house of the property, built in the 1800's, houses the 'River Club Café'. The lagoon frontage allows for an abundance of choice for water-front activities.

***Owner** Rob Knuppe*

35 log chalets, swimming pool, private jetty, water sports by arrangement and conference facilities. Sun Valley Drive, Knysna. P.O. Box 2986, Knysna, 6570.

***phone** 044 382 6483* ***fax** 044 382 6484*

***e-mail** knysna.riverclub@pixie.co.za* ***website** www.knysnariverclub.co.za*

KNYSNA LOG INN ★★★★

KNYSNA

The remarkable log structure of this luxury hotel is the largest in the southern hemisphere. The use of indigenous woods is evident from the spectacular central staircase to the individually hand-carved pillars that adorn the central lobby. Inside, the warmth of this natural feel is complemented by the tasteful fabrics and furniture of the public areas. On the ground floor are a large variety of shops and 'The Logg-Inn Restaurant'.

***General Managers** Peter and Marti Dale*

38 twin rooms, 19 loft suites, swimming pool, jacuzzi, sauna, conference facilities. 16 Gray Street, Knysna. P.O. Box 46, Knysna, 6570.

***phone** 044 382 5835* ***fax** 044 382 5830*

***e-mail** log-inn@mweb.co.za* ***website** www.kli.co.za*

LAGOONA INN ★★★★

KNYSNA

Lagoona Inn was established in 1999 by your hosts Gunter and Alison Pichler, renowned award-winning hoteliers. The style is somewhat Mediterranean, Spanish Caribbean, with a touch of German management. Every one of the 18 bedrooms enjoy spectacular views of the sparkling lagoon surrounded by an amphitheatre of mountains and forests that create a wonderful natural canvas for the first-time visitor. Gould's special note: Gunter and Alison are personal friends and Gunter's cooking is legendary!

***Owners** Gunter and Alison Pichler*
18 rooms, swimming pool, secure parking
George Rex Drive, Knysna. P.O. Box 1488, Knysna, 6570.
***phone** 044 382 4656* ***fax** 044 382 0034*
***e-mail** lagoona@mweb.co.za* ***website** www.lagoona.co.za*

BELVIDERE MANOR ★★★★

KNYSNA

The Belvidere Manor House, which has been superbly restored, is at the heart of 10 acres of well maintained sloping gardens. Individual cottages with fire places, wide verandas and spacious bedrooms all have panoramic views of the Knysna Lagoon, Outeniqua Mountains and the surrounding forests. The Manor House houses the reception, sitting room and dining rooms with splendid yellowwood floors and furnished with Cape antiques.

***General Manager** Sue Mills*
30 cottages, swimming pool.
Belvidere Estate. P.O. Box 1195, Knysna, 6570.
***phone** 044 387 1055* ***fax** 044 387 1059*
***e-mail** manager@belvidere.co.za* ***website** www.belvidere.co.za*

PEZULA

Pezula Golf Estate

Length of Course: *6394 metres*

Type of Course: *Parkland an d Links*

PEZULA

Pezula Country Estate — ***Map reference:*** *23*

Length of Course: *6394 metres (back tees)* ***Holes:*** *18*

Type of Course: *Parkland and Links* ***Par:*** *72*

Visitors: *Private club. Bookings are essential and are on a space availability basis*

Club Professional: *Director of Golf, Jeff Clause*

Tuition: *Yes* ***Club Shop:*** *Yes*

Practice Facilities*: Chipping and putting greens*

Hire Facilities: *Clubs, carts (Carts are recommended and included in the playing fees)*

Catering: *Bar, restaurant, halfway house*

Location: *Lagoonview Drive, Knysna.*

Contact: *Jeff Clause*

Postal address: *P.O.Box 3378, Knysna 6570*

Phone: *044 384 1222* ***Fax:*** *044 384 1277*

e-mail: *golf@pezula.co.za* ***web:*** *www.pezulaclub.com*

A WORLD-CLASS COUNTRY CLUB

The Pezula (formerly Sparrebosch) golf course is situated in one of the most spectacular locations in South Africa. Situated atop the famous Knysna Heads, the high vantage point allows for majestic panoramic views. On one side lies the tranquil Knysna lagoon backed by the Tsitsikama mountain range. On the other side is the ever fascinating Indian Ocean, sometime crashing and sometime lapping onto rugged and dramatic cliffs. Ronald Fream, from the USA, whose classic layouts in sensitive conservation areas have become legendary worldwide, designed the golf course. Here, a protected nature reserve in a hilly landscape of many moods was the challenge. The completed picture has made no compromise to the sensitivity of nature and many of the holes are bound by conservation restrictions. This allows the golfer the bonus of not only enjoying the resulting challenge, but also of savouring the sheer beauty of the indigenous flora and fauna that remain untouched and thriving in their natural habitat.

Where man now follows the paths of the mown fairways to the sensational greens is a complement to this scenic and quite unspoilt landscape.

The course has encompassed the many moods on offer on this varied and hilly terrain. Dramatic downhill holes, backed by the ocean, provide truly unforgettable moments. Classic sweeping fairways winding through forested areas create further drama. Last, but not least, rolling fairways lined by that aforementioned indigenous bush are the arteries that lead to large shapely greens, while allowing vistas of the forests in the distance and the magical lagoon below.

Such beauty is difficult to capture in words. The notices on the tees, advising the player of distances to avoid some of the hazards that are no-go areas and to advise the golfer not to forget to look up and savour the surrounds, show the care and attention to detail around this sensitive environment. This attention continues when noticing the manicuring of the fairways and semi-rough areas and the quality of the putting surfaces. With the nature conservation foremost in mind during the design, some holes here provide different choices from some of the tees. However, on completing a round here, golfers will leave knowing they have played a major challenge, especially if the strong breezes that occasionally appear in this sea-side location, decide to accompany them.

THE COURSE:

The downhill holes of the 12th, 13th and the dramatic short par 4, 14th, are visually never to be forgotten. I will let you savour these, sight unseen. I have chosen three holes to capture the 3 different moods on offer here.

2nd Hole - Par 4 - 343 metres

This hole is a major challenge that begins with a tee shot that has to find a fairway left of a major water feature. This is a hole that offers a feast or famine option off the tee. The brave will decide on a driver and take on fairway bunkers and a tight line close to the water. The more prudent will opt for safety with a long iron avoiding all the hazards. There is a long curving sweep that leads uphill to a well-guarded green. Apart from the water right, indigenous bush left awaits the too cautious bail out shots.

4th Hole - Par 4 - 297 metres

This is a visually spectacular and classic golf hole. Trees line both sides of this hole. The end target is straight ahead but strategically placed fairway bunkers have to be threaded via the fairway that meanders slowly uphill to a superb green. Pin position here is important as the green is large. On the right bunkers await and on the left a grassy bank can throw the intended shot some distance away.

7th Hole - Par 4 - 401 metres

From a high tee the hole is visible all the way to the green. The fairway runs first steeply downhill two thirds of the way, before inclining steeply upward to the green. The fairway is wide though bush on either side intimidates a little. From the tee the longer hitters will hope to catch a steep downhill slope, while the ordinary mortal will be glad to have a shot form a flat lie and to have a moment to savour the lagoon view to the right. There are plenty of hero holes ahead!

8th hole

1st hole

18th hole

PEZULA PRIVATE ESTATE:

The Sparrebosch golf course was developed as the heart of a successful real estate development. Housing now surrounds the many different locations on offer in this pristine environment. This success has now received new impetus, the Pezula Group of Companies has bought the golf course and clubhouse at Sparrebosch.

The motivation comes from American Keith Stewart, whose experienced eye, born of living in some of the world's best locations, and with a passion for Africa, identified this area 'Near the Gods' as something quite exceptional. (Pezula comes from the Shona language and loosely translated means 'Near the Gods'.)

Following the purchase of the golf course and facilities, Keith Stewart and partners have invested into 612 Hectares of former industrial forest bordering the golf course and blessed with forest, beach, cliff top and river locations.

The vision is to develop this into a very low-density housing development, once again adhering to the strict demands of the local environment authorities and to create spectacular facilities to compete with the best of the world's 'Country Clubs'.

Nature Reserve

At present memberships, in the form of a tradeable asset, in a South African Public Company are being sold into the 'Pezula Club', this entitling shareholders not only membership of the golf course (without having to own property), but also access to the planned facilities at Pezula. These will include tennis courts, private swimming pools, an equestrian centre, a beach club and even a sailing club to be housed on the lagoon. The plans also include the introduction of a cricket club! The clubhouse at Pezula is, at the time of writing, being extended to offer a members bar, additional function facilities and an elegant cigar room. Improvements on the golf course have also been implemented, with the introduction of extra irrigation and the fine-tuning of landing areas.

This vision is to be punctuated by a further opportunity to be part of this exceptional Country Club. The cliff top bordering the 14th Hole, overlooking dramatic and rugged cliffs fronting the Indian Ocean below, is the 'Cove'. Here, six prime properties are being developed. The homes on this remarkable location will surely also receive the reputation of being 'Near the Gods'. A 'Nature Reserve' on your doorstep, a championship golf course as a back garden, forest, beach and river within walking distance and for the more energetic, the abundance of facilities of your own private country club. Add to all of this, uninterrupted views of the Indian Ocean. Near the Gods? More like in heaven I think!

Gould's special note:

There is a passion for excellence at this club. This begins with the vision set by Keith Stewart and the attention to detail by the exceptional resident team led by Director of Golf (and fun!) Jeff Clause, his equally active and vibrant wife Liezl and marketing director Hugh O'Shea.

PARKES MANOR HOUSE ★★★★

KNYSNA

Parkes Manor, a stylish country house, is a National Monument, restore to its full glory. The house is situated on a leafy estate of large trees an park-like gardens overlooking the magnificent Knysna lagoon. Spaciou bedrooms are tastefully decorated with wrap-around verandahs wher guests can relax and enjoy the views across the garden and pool are and observe the ever-changing colours of the lagoon. A Health and Beauty centre provides relaxation and anti-ageing treatments.

Owners *Eugene and Chantelle Knoetze*
8 bedrooms, swimming pool, lemana health and beauty centre.
1 Azalia Street, Knysna. P.O. Box 2075, Knysna, 6570.
phone *044 382 5100* **fax** *044 382 5124*
e-mail *parkesmanor@mweb.co.za* **website** *www.parkesmanor.co.za*

LAKE PLEASANT ★★★★★

KNYSNA

The 5-star Lake Pleasant Hotel & Spa is situated on the banks of Groenvle the only freshwater lake in the area, and amidst the bird sanctuary of the adjacent Goukamma Nature & Marine Reserve. The 36 en-suite, beautifull appointed bedrooms all have views over the lake and indigenous, landscape garden. The "Top 100" Restaurant serves breakfast, lunch and dinner an is open to the public. The well-equipped Wellness Centre offers a range of treatments, enabling guests to relax, rejuvenate and be pampered.

General Manager *Vanessa Weyers*
36 rooms, swimming pool, wellness centre, conference facilities.
On the N2 - Groenvlei, between George and Knysna. P.O. Box 3530, Knysna, 6570.
phone *044 349 2400* **fax** *044 349 2401*
e-mail *info@lakepleasanthotel.com* **website** *www.lakepleasanthotel.com*

PLETTENBERG BAY

Plettenberg Bay Golf Course

Length of Course: *5926 metres*

Type of Course: *Parkland*

PLETTENBERG BAY

Plettenberg Bay Golf Course | **Map reference:** *24*
Length of Course: *5926 metres* | **Holes:** *18*
Type of Course: *Parkland* | **Par:** *72*
Visitors: *No restrictions*
Club Professional: *No*
Tuition: *Yes* | **Club Shop:** *Yes*
Practice Facilities: *Putting greens*
Hire Facilities: *Clubs, trolleys and drive carts (bookings essential)*
Catering: *Bar, halfway house*
Location: *Piesang Valley, Plettenberg Bay*
Contact: *Jeanette Bloem*
Postal address: *P.O.Box 92, Plettenberg Bay 6600*
Phone: *044 533 2132* | **Fax:** *044 533 0035*
e-mail: *pbcc@global.co.za* | **web:** *www.plettgolf.co.za*

PLEASANT VALLEY

Nestled in the Piesang Valley, some five kilometres from the outstanding Plettenberg Bay beaches, is the Plettenberg Bay Golf Club. This is a charming resort golf course that has, over recent years, undergone a well-orchestrated upgrading programme. None of the charm has been lost and you can now enjoy a quality course with the Piesang River meandering through the course and a host of different tree and bird species.

The two opening holes (1st and 10th) are straight downhill with the 10th turning sharply to the right. The two finishing holes (9th and 18th) climb their way back to the single-storey clubhouse overlooking the scenic valley.

The golf course is always busy at Christmas and Easter, as Plettenberg Bay is one of South Africa's major holiday destinations. However, as I am repeatedly reminded that visitors are always welcome, I have no doubt that you will enjoy both the welcome that you will receive and your round of golf on this hilly, well laid out resort course.

Gould's special note:

This course has developed remarkably, despite its small budget. Much of this was the responsibility of former golf professional Mike Ness, who was at the club for many years. I especially enjoy the fact that the lake on the course has been named "Loch Ness"!

Added to the course improvements are the very noticeable quality features that have been introduced at the clubhouse, including a delightful terrace allowing splendid views of the area and the course below.

THE COURSE

4th Hole - Par 5 - 480 metres

As you stand on this tee, you will also notice the wide, well-shaped fairway and although trouble lurks both to the left and the right, you will have to work at a bad shot to get there. The real interest lies in the third shot to the green fronted by the river and protected by a long bunker right. A back bunker will catch those of you who are overly cautious about missing the water.

7th Hole - Par 5 - 434 metres

At the bottom of the valley, a long, thin tee leads to a narrow fairway with a solitary tree on the left, narrowing the perspective even further. The Piesang River runs along to the right. Long hitters will be tempted to go for the green in two. It is advisable to hug the sloping left bank as anything pushed might rejoin the river. Avoid hitting too far left, however as you will find yourself in the midst of trees and thick rough. The green has a high bank behind it and a back bunker to the right. A small, flat bunker on the front left may surprise you!

14th Hole - Par 4 - 276 metres

This is a really unusual golf hole. With the whispering yellowwoods that back onto the tee, you could easily imagine yourself in the rain forests of East Africa. The hole doglegs to the left and turns uphill past two majestic oak trees, reputedly over 200 years old. A bank sloping from right to left will stop too long a shot from the tee. You only need a long iron or short wood to hit the right hand side of the fairway thus ensuring a straight shot to the uphill green. Alternatively you may need a high loft over the oaks to reach this green closely guarded by four bunkers.

THE AREA

Safe swimming and golden beaches, in addition to year-round good weather, explain why Plettenberg Bay is such a popular resort. Water sports abound, with sailing, diving and deep sea fishing forming part of everyday life. There are also lagoons where water skiing, boating and canoeing are ever-popular. If all this activity is slightly daunting to you, you might like to simply relax at one of the beach front hotels and may be lucky enough to be there when the whales are calving. For me, (a fashionable eco-tourist) the pleasure of spending time in this area is the variety of bird life, with more than 200 species.

THE PLETTENBERG ★★★★★

PLETTENBERG BAY

The Plettenberg, built on a rocky headland with breathtaking vistas of sea, mountains and miles of golden sand, is situated in one of the most spectacular resorts in Africa - Plettenberg Bay. Experience fabulous sightings of dolphins. From June to September whales can be spotted in the bay. Walk along miles of pristine beaches or relax in one of the two heated swimming pools. 37 luxury rooms and suites offer a truly idyllic and indulgent experience. A Relais et Châteaux Hotel.

General Manager *Nigel Pace*
37 rooms, 2 swimming pools, restaurant, spa and beauty salon
40 Church Street. P.O. Box 719, Plettenberg Bay, 6600.
phone *044 533 2030* **fax** *044 533 2074*
e-mail *plettenberg@pixie.co.za* **website** *www.collectionmcgrath.com*

PERIWINKLE GUEST LODGE ★★★★

PLETTENBERG BAY

Periwinkle Lodge is located 10 minutes from the Plettenberg Airport and offers you a breathtaking seafront experience. All en-suite rooms have private patios with spectacular views over the ocean. The rooms are equipped with Tea/Coffee making facilities, television and mini-bar. This is a truly unique experience for the discerning traveller. Your home away from home.

General manager *Colleen Basson*
7 rooms, 75 Beachy Head Drive, Plettenberg Bay.
P.O.Box 881, Plettenberg Bay, 6600.
phone *044 533 1345* **fax** *044 533 1345*
e-mail *res@periwinklelodge.co.za* **website** *www.periwinklelodge.co.za*

GOOSE VALLEY

Goose Valley Golf Course
Length of Course: *5880 metres*
Type of Course: *Links*
Holes: *18*
Par: *72*

GOOSE VALLEY

Goose Valley Golf Course | ***Map reference:*** *10*
Length of Course: *5880 metres* | ***Holes:*** *18*
Type of Course: *Links* | ***Par:*** *72*
Visitors: *Booking essential in season*
Club Professional: *Jannie Viljoen*
Tuition: *Yes* | ***Club Shop:*** *Yes 044 533 5082*
Practice Facilities: *Putting greens and driving range*
Hire Facilities: *Clubs, trolleys and drive carts*
Catering: *Bar, restaurant and halfway house*
Location: *N2 Highway, 1.8km outside Plettenberg Bay towards Port Elizabeth*
Contact: *Errol Walsh*
Postal address: *P O Box 448, Plettenberg Bay 6600*
Phone: *044 533 0846* | ***Fax:*** *044 533 0847*
e-mail: *goose.valley@pixie.co.za* | ***web:*** *www.goosevalley.net*

TURTLE CREEK

At the time of writing this, October 2002, the Goose Valley golf course is busy expanding from a superb nine holes to an exceptional 18 holes. I can safely say this as I have walked the new holes, designed by Gary Player Design Company, to complement the scenic 9 holes that have become renowned for their tight challenge and visual beauty. The new nine has sweeping fairways around wonderful water hazards, large and undulating greens and provides a series of different moods. Tree-lined fairways are interspersed with open and uncluttered landscape and the rise and fall of the natural undulating terrain adds much to the variety and flow of classic and challenging holes.

The expansion from 9 to 18 holes is as a result of a new real estate development phase. This is the Turtle Creek Estate and it has proved itself a success even prior to the new golf holes being opened for play. This is not surprising in an area of the Garden Route known for its temperate climate, its spectacular beaches and secure, holiday atmosphere. The housing estate apart, the expansion of the Goose Valley Club includes substantial improvements to the clubhouse and general facilities and without doubt, both the visitor and the permanent resident will cherish the quality and style that has resulted from the expansion.

What will remain the same, and in no need of improvement, is the manicuring of this layout among a protected and sensitive nature reserve blessed with sensational sea views and indigenous fynbos. That the protection of this environment is of paramount importance is reflected in the fact that golf balls straying into the reserve area are to be declared lost. Your reaction to this inconvenience will be softened as you are also made aware, by the constant signs around the course, of the need to 'Beware of the Snakes'

The original nine holes have set a standard for the completed 18 holes. Immaculate fairways and first class greens are complemented by the splendour of this natural environment. Truly memorable though, will be the sparkling vistas of the Indian Ocean that may distract you from the focus needed to maximize the joy of playing Gary Player's 18 holes. Interestingly, the golf course and the estate have been designed around Gary Player's original home here. That Mr. Player understands quality living will without doubt become apparent whether visiting Goose Valley for the first time, or staying more permanently at Turtle Creek.

THE COURSE

Though the new nine holes are near completion at the time of publishing my guide, I will introduce the course with the existing opening three holes.

1st Hole - Par 4 - 370 metres

This hole sets the tone for your experience at Goose Valley. Dense vegetation lines the left and right and you will be searching for a narrow fairway made narrower by the bunkers on either side. A slight dogleg left, the fairway leads uphill to a large sloping green with subtle slopes and different tiers.

2nd Hole - Par 3 - 152 metres

It is on this tee that you will get a sense of the visual beauty of the area. A glorious par three starts from an elevated tee overlooking dense foliage with the green below. Six bunkers surround a wide and narrow target. A lagoon and the sea are the backdrops to enhance the total picture.

3rd Hole - Par 4 - 315 metres

From this tee only think about avoiding the well-shaped fairway bunkers that guard your progress to this short par 4. There are three bunkers right and two left. Once these have been negotiated, a short iron is required to a two-tiered green with two bunkers as sentries.

ASTRON RESORT ★★★★

PLETTENBERG BAY

Nestled on a private estate embraced by the Indian Ocean, the Keurbooms River and the rolling fairways of Goose Valley Golf Course, this contemporary African hotel offers luxury accommodation in the heart of the Garden Route. Share their warm hospitality in the African bar or taste the finest of local and international flavours at the Illanga Restaurant. Gould's special note: The hotel, recently bought by NH Hotels, a group out of Spain, will change its brand name in the year 2003.

General Manager *Marijke Louw*

37 rooms, 5 luxury suites, swimming pool. On the N2 - next to Goose Valley Golf Estate. P.O. Box 2435, Plettenberg Bay, 6600.

phone *044 533 3572* **fax** *044 533 3582*

e-mail *astronresort.plett@mweb.co.za* **website** *www.nh-hotels.co.za*

KURLAND ★★★★★

PLETTENBERG BAY

Set amidst emerald green pastures at the foothills of the Outeniqua Mountains, and surrounded by paddocks, meadows and immaculate polo fields, lies Kurland, a tranquil estate and luxurious country hotel. Individually styled rooms each have a magnificent bathroom, living area, couches, satellite television and mini bars. Be indulged in sumptuous meals and fine wines, recline at the pool, relax in a deep chair or be pampered in the spa.

General Manager *Jonitha McKenzie*

12 rooms (10 family suites and 2 bedrooms), swimming pool, spa, tennis, horse back riding, polo pavilion. P.O. Box 209, The Crags, 6602.

phone *044 534 8082* **fax** *044 534 8699*

e-mail *info@kurland.co.za* **website** *www.kurland.co.za*

GOOSE VALLEY
GOLF ESTATE - PLETTENBERG BAY

**NOW
18 HOLES**

The Goose Valley Golf Estate is situated in pristine surroundings, only 2km from Plettenberg Bay and bordering on the Keurbooms Lagoon. This new magnificent golf estate offers golfers a Gary Player designed 72 par, 18-hole golf course in the heart of the Garden Route. Golfers will experience breathtaking views of the lagoon, the ocean and the Tsistikamma Mountains, as also the beauty of the natural fynbos, trees and an abundance of animal and bird life.

The new clubhouse includes a spacious upmarket restaurant and state-of-the-art proshop within a warm and friendly environment created by a great team of staff and teaching professionals. The estate is further enhanced by an abundance of natural water and a Driving Range and practice chipping and putting facilities.

The jewel in the crown is the new Turtle Creek freehold housing estate within the Goose Valley Resort, where plots have sold prolifically and houses are being constructed according to a strict design plan.

telephone +27(44) 533 5082 **fax** +27(44) 533 0847
e-mail goose.valley@pixie.co.za
P.O.Box 448 Plettenberg Bay 6600.
website www.goosevalley.net

PORT ELIZABETH

Port Elizabeth Golf Course — ***Map reference:*** *37*
Length of Course: *6117 metres* — ***Holes:*** *18*
Type of Course: *Parkland* — ***Par:*** *72*
Visitors: *Booking essential*
Club Professional: *Graham Whale 041 373 1212*
Tuition: *Yes* — ***Club Shop:*** *Yes*
Practice Facilities: *Yes - own balls, putting greens*
Hire Facilities: *Clubs, trolleys, caddies and drive carts*
Catering: *Bar, restaurant, halfway house*
Location: *Westview Drive, Mill Park*
Contact: *Rob Orchard*
Postal address: *P.O.Box 27985, Green Acres 6057*
Phone: *041 374 3140* — ***Fax:*** *041 374 3276*
e-mail: *pegolf@mweb.co.za* — ***web:*** *www.pegolf.co.za*

THE HILL

Any club that has been in existence for over 100 years is bound to be steeped in tradition and the Port Elizabeth Golf Club, known to locals as "The Hill", is such a club. You only have to spend a few minutes reading the honours boards to realise this.

The honours boards are hung in the recently renovated and truly spacious clubhouse. Improvements have also taken place on the golf course in recent times.

If you combine the above mentioned elements with the fact that the club is located in the "Friendly City", as Port Elizabeth is known, you will easily imagine the kind of welcome that you will receive.

The golf course itself adds value to your experience here as it provides some truly challenging tests of your golfing skills. This 18-hole parkland course has spectacular garden features and the recently redesigned greens provide the visitor with the only Putter bent grass greens in the greater Port Elizabeth area. The fairways meander along an undulating layout through a variety of trees - the most noticeable being the colourful coral trees, indigenous to the region.

THE COURSE

15th Hole - Par 4 - 408 metres

Although trees line both sides of the fairway, there is a wide expanse of cut fairway to aim for. This long hole doglegs right, so most players tend to aim for the left. The longer hitters can go over the trees on the right hand side. This provides an easier shot to a difficult sloping green. Accuracy is paramount no matter where the pin is placed. The green is also guarded by three deep bunkers, two on the right and one front left.

16th Hole - Par 4 - 304 metres

This gentle par 4 is again tree-lined, but there is a fairly wide fairway which slopes upwards to yet another rolling green. Two bunkers guard the green and no less than five fairway bunkers need to be avoided. The danger is playing an approach too long, because the return putt is on a surface that slopes sharply back towards the fairway.

17th Hole - Par 3 - 154 metres

This is the Hill's 'Signature Hole' and features on the cover of the club's scorecard. It is a picturesque and tough short hole which has a difficult sloping green guarded by a bunker left and water right. Even a slightly mis-directed shot can often get wet! Magnificent palm trees stand like sentinels on guard at the back of the green, adding to the visual splendour of the hole.

THE AREA

Port Elizabeth was named by the Governor of the Cape Sir Rofane Donkin, after his wife Elizabeth, who had died in India. The old fort, built in 1799 by the British army, ranks as the oldest stone building in the Eastern Cape and offers a good view over the harbour and along the coastline.

A walking tour of the city on the Donkin Heritage Trail is a good way to take in some of the history and places of interest including churches, monuments and gardens. One statue that few visitors miss is the Horse Memorial, erected in 1905 as a monument to the many horses that died during the Anglo-Boer War. This empathetic work depicts a rider kneeling to give water to his thirsty horse. It is one of the rare memorials in the world built specifically to honour the memory of horses.

HUMEWOOD

Humewood Golf Course

Length of Course: *5935 metres*

Type of Course: *Links*

Holes: *18*

Par: *72*

HUMEWOOD

Humewood Golf Course
Map reference: 36
Length of Course: 5935 metres
Holes: 18
Type of Course: Links
Par: 72
Visitors: Bookings Wednesday, Saturday, Sunday
Club Professional: Greg Thomas 041 583 2256
Tuition: Yes
Club Shop: Yes
Practice Facilities: Putting greens, driving range
Hire Facilities: Clubs, trolleys, caddies and drive carts
Catering: Bar, restaurant,
Location: Marine Drive, Strand
General Manager: Garth Webster
Postal address: P.O.Box 13165, Humewood, 6013
Phone: 041 583 2137
Fax: 041 583 1775
e-mail: info@humewoodgolf.co.za
web: www.humewoodgolf.co.za

CROWNED PLOVER

The first thing that strikes you on arrival at this course is the stately, double-storey, white clubhouse from which you have marvellous views of the course and the bay. The Humewood course was designed by the English course architect, Colonel S.V. Hotchkins, and is deservedly regarded as his finest piece of work. A testament to this is that the club has hosted the South African Open Championships on no less than 9 occasions.

It is a links course with wide rolling fairways featuring numerous mounds and hollows. As is the case with most coastal courses, wind plays a big role and the par of some of the holes often depends on which wind is blowing! The winds can sometimes reach ferocious proportions and this certainly adds to what is already a testing and challenging course.

The terrain along the course is rugged with indigenous fynbos vegetation and an abundance of wildlife. Crowned Plovers live on the course and often nest on the fairways but you will know to avoid their homes as they are marked with red flags.

Gould's special note:

'Gulf Green' cynodon grass has been introduced to the greens, and this has proved ideal for the sea-side weather patterns here.

THE COURSE

1st Hole - Par 4 - 356 metres

The first hole captures the essence of Humewood. To your right is the splendid clubhouse that sets the tone for a magnificent golfing challenge. As you line up your tee shot, you will see a rolling fairway with fynbos and bushes as well as the sea in the distance. The degree of difficulty here is dictated by the strength of the wind. Your second shot is to a green protected by swales to the left and a bank to the right. Bush both at the back and right awaits you if your shot is too long.

13th Hole - Par 4 - 399 metres

Rolling and meandering its way through the local bush is the tough par 4, 13th hole. The main difficulty here lies in hitting your second shot to an elevated green. A high bank situated short right presents a tricky, sandy lie if you are too short. A deep bunker sitting short left will stop your ball from sliding further away from the green. I suggest that you favour the right as crescent shaped slopes will help your ball back to the green.

18th Hole - Par 4 - 358 metres

No matter how you have played up until now (or if you caught Humewood on a windy day), the sight of the clubhouse in the distance will have you relishing the golfing tradition. The fairway here features substantial mounds and you should aim for the highest part of the clubhouse from the tee. The second shot requires taking on two large bunkers short right of the green that will catch a fade and two smaller, but no less penalising ones, will welcome the pulled shot.

THE AREA

The 'Boardwalk' is the latest development to grace the Port Elizabeth beach front. This exceptionally well-planned development, centres around a casino complex and offers a choice of restaurants, shops and an abundance of vibrant eating outlets. A sparkling water feature sits at the heart of this development and while charming during the day, it shimmers to the lighting system at night. Another prime tourist attraction is the Oceanarium. This features a museum of natural history and shipwrecks, a snake park housing a thousand reptiles, aquarium and dolphinarium. The complex, with its spectacular leaping dolphins, attracts 16000 visitors a year.

From the harbour runs a narrow gauge steam train that brings in fruit from the Avontuur Valley. But on Saturdays, from June to January, it takes passengers on its quaint journey over gorges and into rugged mountain scenery.

Surfing can be enjoyed at various beaches but perhaps none so much as at Jeffrey's Bay with its legendary waves. Exotic shells are often found on beach walks. A short drive north across Sunday's River is a reserve of dense bush with beard-like strands of moss and lichen. It is the favourite food of the Addo elephant and here they roam at will with buffalo, black rhino and other game. Catch them at one of the watering holes.

PAXTON HOTEL ★★★★

PORT ELIZABETH

This modern venue has a superb location overlooking the harbour and is only 10 minutes away from the airport. It is also within easy walking distance of the city centre, the Boardwalk and the beach. The sea frontage has prompted a 'wave' theme throughout the hotel and this is carried through the spacious en-suite rooms to the pool, lounge, bar and dining areas. The emphasis here is on traditional values-service to the guests. Only 5km away from Humewoods famous Links course.

Managing Director *Werner Peterseil*
79 rooms, 1 suite, swimming pool, conference facilities.
Carnarvon Place, Humerail. P.O. Box 13737, Humewood, 6013.
phone *041 585 9655* **fax** *041 585 9640*
e-mail *paxton@iafrica.com* **website** *www.paxton.co.za*

SUMMERSTRAND INN ★★★

PORT ELIZABETH

This large hotel has truly managed to blend a sense of the personal touch with the amenities required of the international traveller. Summerstrand is owner-managed and the attention to detail is evident throughout the property, especially in the spacious en-suite rooms, which are tastefully decorated. There are 2 bars; a 150-seater restaurant and a delightful Mediterranean lounge overlooking the gardens and sparkling pool area. There are magnificent views of the sea and the Humewood golf course.

Owner *Mark Hartman*
230 rooms, swimming pool, tennis, conference facilities.
Marine Drive, Summerstrand. P.O. Box 204, Port Elizabeth, 6000.
phone *041 583 3131* **fax** *041 583 2505*
e-mail *hotsummer@icon.co.za* **website** *www.hotsummer.co.za*

FISH RIVER

Fish River Golf Estate

Length of Course: *6298 metres*

Type of Course: *Coastal*

Holes: *18*

Par: *72*

FISH RIVER

Fish River Golf Estate ***Map reference:*** *35*
Length of Course: *6298 metres* ***Holes:*** *18*
Type of Course: *Coastal* ***Par:*** *72*
Visitors: *No restrictions*
Club Professional: *Graeme Matthews*
Tuition: *Yes* ***Club Shop:*** *Yes*
Practice Facilities: *Yes - own balls, putting greens*
Hire Facilities: *Clubs, trolleys and drive carts*
Catering: *Bar, restaurant, halfway house*
Location: *Halfway between Port Elizabeth and East London*
General Manager: *Graeme Mathews*
Postal address: *P.O.Box 232, Port Alfred, 6170*
Phone: *040 676 1002* ***Fax:*** *040 676 1115*
e-mail: *fishsun@sunint.co.za* ***web:*** *www.sunint.co.za*

OLD WOMAN'S RIVER

The Eastern Cape coastline is dramatic with dense vegetation and windswept, unspoilt beaches. Gary Player, who designed the Fish River course, made full use of the natural surroundings and terrain and he has produced a golf course which combines drama, beauty and ruggedness to provide an excellent golfing challenge. The indigenous Euphorbia trees, which are almost cactus-like in appearance, were left untouched and preside over many of the holes.

The Old Woman's River, which you will cross twice via a river bridge, needs to be carried on both the 13th and 16th holes. On this course you will find yourself contending with bushy dunes and you may have to cope with the windy conditions that are so much part of this coastal region. The Kikuyu fairways are always in good condition and in recent years the original bayview greens have been replaced with quite superb bent grass greens. Water is in rather short supply in this region, but careful planning and the high standards set by the Fish River team, have resulted in this golf course receiving accolades for its year-round quality.

The Fish River course is part of the Fish River Sun Hotel and Country Club Resort. Here you can enjoy a multitude of sports facilities as well as rock fishing and deep-sea fishing nearby.

THE COURSE

12 Hole - Par 5 - 456 metres

The river dominates the left hand side, while the rolling fairway sweeps around the river bend from left to right. Your tee shot is to a narrow fairway and your second shot has to avoid a thicket of trees that create a narrow gap between them and the river. The fairway rises steeply to a green that is protected by a solitary tree on the left. Long hitters will have to cut across the water and the bush to the left of the green could come in to play.

13th Hole - Par 4 - 391 metres

The river runs below you on this tee and your shot has to carry the water to an elevated fairway some distance away. You will need to cross the river via a memorable bridge in order to rejoin the ball. Trouble lies on the left where a large, kidney-shaped green is guarded by three pot bunkers to the right.

14th Hole - Par 4 - 341 metres

A narrow avenue of trees guides you to the ideal landing spot for your ball on this sharp dogleg. The second shot is to a wide green that appears to be surrounded by trees. There are, in fact, only three trees but swales and bunkers will add to your problems.

THE AREA

It is in this area of the Great Fish River that black met white. This was frontier territory where the western civilisation came face to face with primitive Africa. The river marked the divide of understanding and ignorance of the people living on the other side led to legendary stories and myths about the ways of the mystery people - and to a succession of frontier wars. This is an open undulating area of rolling grassy hills and densely forested mountains. It is given to good agricultural land with its sub-tropical climate and rich soil. Amongst other crops, pineapples set this area apart from the landscape of the other parts of the Cape: vast fields cover hilly slopes. The beginnings of the plantations were in a barber's shop in 1865 where the barber had the spike tops growing in glass jars of water in his shop (like scalped heads) as a curiosity and conversation piece for his customers. One customer, a farmer, took some home and found that they flourished in these conditions. At the Fish River you can enjoy walks along unspoilt beaches, breakfast with the sun shimmering off the Indian Ocean and a glass of very fresh pineapple juice!

FISH RIVER SUN

EASTERN CAPE

The Fish River Sun is at the heart of a leisure resort blessed with an abundance of recreational opportunities. Tennis, squash, bowls; mini-golf, rock and surf fishing and deep-sea fishing are some of the choices. Add to this the Gary Player designed championship golf course set against the dramatic ocean backdrop, and you have fun filled days. The luxurious self-catering apartments can be used alternatively as normal hotel rooms.

Operations Manager *Wessel Benson*

40 luxurious self catering units, swimming pool, conference facilities. R72 national Road

P.O. Box 232, Port Alfred, 6170.

phone *040 676 1101* ***fax*** *040 676 1115*

e-mail *fishsun@sunint.co.za* ***website*** *www.fishriversun.co.za*

ROYAL PORT ALFRED

Royal Port Alfred Golf Course
Map reference: *38*
Length of Course: *5771 metres*
Holes: *18*
Type of Course: *Links*
Par: *72*
Visitors: *No restrictions*
Club Professional: *No*
Tuition: *No*
Club Shop: *Yes*
Practice Facilities*: Putting Green*
Hire Facilities: *None*
Catering: *Bar, halfway house (open Wednesdays and Saturdays)*
Location: *St Andrew Road, Port Alfred*
Contact: *Mike Atterbury*
Postal address: *P.O.Box 418, Port Alfred 6170*
Phone: *046 624 4796*
Fax: *046 624 4388*
e-mail: *rpagc@border.co.za*

WIND AND HUMPS

The Port Alfred Golf Course was constructed between 1907 and 1915, receiving its royal status from King George V through the Governor General of the Union, Prince Arthur of Connaught, in 1924.

During the 1920's, the course was extremely popular as it was one of the few links courses accessible by rail, and most holiday-makers in those days travelled by train. It was said at that time, "You are not a golfer until you have beaten the Royal Port Alfred".

The course has undergone many changes since its early beginnings and has experienced many difficulties through the decades due to lack of funding, although the incredible tenacity displayed by club and committee members alike has kept the course open and flourishing through the lean times. The hilly terrain enables you to enjoy beautiful views of both the coastal area and the inland countryside and you would do well to take a breather now and again to enjoy these. Not only will you have to contend with a multitude of humps throughout the course, but the wind factor common to coastal courses plays a large role here. The vegetation is predominantly low bush and dune forest and with the hilly nature of the course, I can guarantee that you will be adopting sloping stances on many of the holes.

Gould's Special Note:

Juan (photographer) and I were privileged to enjoy the company of several buck during our last visit. Quite remarkably they followed our progress over several holes.

THE COURSE

3rd Hole - Par 4 -292 metres

If you look to the left, there is a wonderful view of the Port Alfred sand dunes and beach. The tee shot is to an uphill fairway and, upon reaching the rise, you will feel as if you are hitting into the sea. The green is small and suspended and too long a shot will see your ball running downhill. There are two bunkers on the right to be avoided.

4th Hole - Par 4 - 278 metres

Once again this hole involves a tee shot to an uphill fairway with wide, open spaces to assist you. There is a slight dogleg right and two fairway bunkers will only pose a problem to long hitters. A large bunker on the right seems to be the only hazard at the green but beware of a small left hand bunker concealed by a fairway bunker.

5th Hole - Par 4 - 413 metres

This is another blind tee shot straight towards the sea. Once over the hill, you will find yourself on your way down a sharp hill to the green. The green is small and round and your only concern is the deep grass bunker on the left.

THE AREA

This beautiful seaside resort is located on the banks of the Kowie River. The 1820 Settlers had hoped to use the river mouth as a landing spot for supplies arriving from Algoa Bay, but the mouth proved too difficult to negotiate and they had to abandon the idea. Port Alfred, with its relaxed atmosphere and beautiful surroundings, is a popular holiday destination and is especially loved by surfers who flock to the long beaches to ride the waves. These beaches extend for miles making them ideal for walking. Another popular pastime is that of shell collecting, with over 1800 different varieties having been picked up on the beaches here over the years. The Indian Ocean offers safe swimming in its warm waters.

Port Alfred is an important fishing port and if you head for the river when the boats come in you will be able to choose from a wide variety of delicious fish on sale.

Nearly the Last Word.

Golf Carts: *In recent years many of the clubs have introduced self drive golf carts. It is prudent to book these in advance as they have become popular especially with visiting tourists.*

Caddies: *Caddies are available at most golf clubs in the Cape. A national caddy training program has been in operation for some time, and caddies are graded according to their experience. The rates for the caddy fees are available at the pro-shops. It is customary to add a tip to the official fee and to give something for the halfway-house refreshment.*

Halfway House. *Most golf clubs in South Africa have a halfway house offering refreshment after nine holes. Food and beverage is available and it is customary to take no more than 10 minutes for this sensible pastime.*

Sandbags: *Divots are not replaced in South Africa. Instead, sand is placed in the divot mark. This allows the grass to knit back into place. Sandbags are available for hire or purchase at all the clubs.*

Sun Protection: *South Africa has a very high rate of skin cancer. This is due to the severity of the sun's rays and it is highly recommended that sun protection is a priority before playing a round of golf.*

Spikes: *Most of the golf courses in the Cape require that soft spikes are used.*

19th Hole: *The worldwide tradition of enjoying the 19th hole is very much part of golf in South Africa. If you are participating in a competition it is etiquette to remain for the prize giving.*

Golf Magazines: *There are 3 excellent golf magazines in South Africa. These are: The Compleat Golfer (yes the spelling is correct!) –The Golf Digest Magazine—and Golf Today. These are available in most pro-shops and selected bookstores.*

My final word: *If you have read the introduction to this guide you will know that I am a former hotelier. My background lends itself to giving service to the customer. Should you need any assistance, during or prior to your visit, kindly do not hesitate to contact me either on email (gouldgolf@global.co.za) or at my offices 021 701 7860. Allow me once more to wish you continued joy with the wonderful game of golf---and the joy of the 'off course' experiences to be savoured in this marvellous part of the world.*

East London Golf Course **Map reference:** *34*
Length of Course: *6038 metres* **Holes:** *18*
Type of Course: *Links/parkland* **Par:** *73*
Visitors: *Booking essential*
Club Professional: *No*
Tuition: *Yes* **Club Shop:** *Yes*
Practice Facilities: *Putting and chipping greens*
Hire Facilities: *Clubs, trolleys, caddies and drive carts*
Catering: *Bar, halfway house*
Location: *Gleneagles Road, Bunkers Hill, East London*
Contact: *Daan van Deventer (G.M.) or Radley Dijkers (assist.)*
Postal address: *P.O.Box 226, East London 5200*
Phone: *043 735 1356* **Fax:** *043 735 2426*
e-mail: *info@eastlondongc.co.za* **web:** *www.eastlondongc.co.za*

ROLLER COASTER

Your first good look at this course will be from the clubhouse's high terraced lounge overlooking the 18th green. It is at this moment that you will notice the rolling, undulating fairways of the East London Golf Course and you will, no doubt, realise that you are in for a roller coaster ride! Roller coaster rides are always exciting and challenging, guaranteed to leave you breathless, and this one is no exception! The steep climbs will take you to vantage points from which spectacular views of the Indian Ocean and beachfront add to the scenic splendour of this course.

The fairways meander through dense bush and though the course is in immaculate condition, the terrain still has an overall rugged feel. Dogleg holes and well-guarded, sloping greens are featured and the wind factor, as is typical of the area, is often of concern.

The East London course is one of the oldest courses in the country, dating back to 1893. It has, for many years, featured as one of South Africa's leading courses and although no longer used by professionals in the circuit due to these tournaments now being held only in the major cities, it regularly hosts top amateur competitions.

Various improvements have been effected over recent years, including the thinning out of the bush lining the fairways, and the introduction of a water reticulation system that has resulted in a lusher course.

THE COURSE

2nd Hole - Par 3 - 151 metres

Each hole on this course has its own name and this one is called "The Drop". A high tee gives you a view to the left of the narrow beach stretching to Gonubie and your focus will be downwards to a round green with no less than six bunkers surrounding it. Here, club selection is dependent on the wind and you will choose between a 3 iron and a 9 iron.

7th Hole - Par 4 - 340 metres

Again, this is a high tee that looks at a fairway sloping from left to right. Here you can risk a big drive as your only problems are a thicket of trees, placed short right, and easily avoidable bunkers. Keep your tee shot to the left of centre. Your second shot is towards a pear shaped green where you have five bunkers to negotiate.

9th Hole - Par 4 - 425 metres

This intimidating and spectacular par 4 is my favourite hole on this course. Your tee shot will be to a sloping fairway over a hill that sends your ball into a valley. The hole doglegs left and your target is a long narrow green with a bunker left and a tricky little pot bunker to the right.

THE AREA

East London's scenic beauty is due to its seaside location and rolling hills and valleys. Here you will find superb beaches. The most renowned is Nahoon Beach, most famous in surfing circles. A good way to discover the Nahoon Reef is to have a walk along Gonubie's Boardwalk. The East London river port is on the mouth of the Buffalo River and has in recent years seen a revival of its ship repairing industry. A stop at "Latimers Landing" will provide food and drinks before a boat trip or sail around the harbour. The township of Mdantsane - second only in size to Soweto in Johannesburg - allows for daily tours to experience township life and explore some of the fascinating Xhosa cultural traditions.

The Museum is the home of the Coelacanth and the world's only Dodo egg and shoppers will enjoy a wander through the Lock Street Goal shopping complex - formerly a prison built in the 1800's, at that time South Africa's finest women's jail.

BLUE LAGOON ★★★

EAST LONDON

This hotel has a true resort feel with views of wide-open beaches and glorious blue water. Accommodation is in self-contained units that have rich and vibrant décor to complement the spacious and very well equipped en-suite rooms. The Sunset restaurant, set against the backdrop of the Nahoon River, provides outstanding meals in really attractive surroundings. The hotel's location is ideal for the holidaymaker and the businessman alike.

General Manager *Derek Carroll*
88 rooms, swimming pool.
Blue Bend Place. P.O. Box 2177, Beacon Bay, 5205.
phone *043 748 4821* ***fax*** *043 748 2037*
e-mail *blhotel@iafrica.com* ***website*** *www.bluelagoonhotel.co.za*

HEMINGWAYS ★★★★

EAST LONDON

Situated at the Hemingways casino and entertainment complex in East London, the new luxury Hemingways Hotel offers a relaxed yet sophisticated island lifestyle with architecture and decor inspired by the Key West home of author Ernest Hemingway. Managed by Southern Sun, the hotel is aimed mainly at the corporate market, but the link to the entertainment and casino complex makes it an ideal leisure destination as well.

General Manager *Steve Chimana*
67 rooms, 2 suites, 1 presidential suite, swimming pool, conference facilities.
Corner Two Rivers Drive and Western Bypass-Cambridge. P.O.Box 1950 East London 5200
phone *043 707 8000* ***fax*** *043 707 8010*
e-mail *stevec@southernsun.com* ***website*** *www.southernsun.com*

INDEX where to play

18 HOLE COURSES

These are 18 hole courses that have not been featured in the book

Alexander	*043 736 3646*
Cradock	*048 881 2033*
Grahamstown	*046 622 2106*
Humansdorp	*042 291 0569*
King Williams Town	*043 642 3939*
St Francis Bay	*042 294 0467*
Queenstown	*045 838 4099*
Uitenhage	*041 966 1021*
Walmer	*041 581 1613*
Wedgewood	*041 372 1212*
West Bank	*043 731 1523*

9 HOLE COURSES

These are 9 hole courses that have not been featured in the book

Adelaide	046 684 0489
Albertinia	028 735 1646
Alexandria	046 653 0207
Bedford	046 685 0123
Berg River	022 783 0535
Boggomsbaai	044 699 1163
Bonnievale	023 616 2613
Bredasdorp	028 424 1855
Caledon	028 212 1931
Cathcart	045 843 1014
Ceres	023 312 3068
Citrusdal	022 921 2544
Clanwilliam	027 482 1618
Darling	022 492 2684
Dirkie Fourie	053 963 1115
De Hoek	022 913 1926
Dordrecht	045 943 1673
Fort Beaufort	046 645 1959
Gansbaai	028 384 1441
Hankey	042 284 0335
Heidelberg	028 722 1573
Helderberg Village	021 855 1200
Hex Valley	023 356 3379
Jeffreys Bay	042 293 2532
Kirkwood	042 230 0452
Kleinmond	028 271 3525
Komga	043 831 1069
Ladismith	028 551 2568
Laingsburg	023 551 1040
Lamberts Bay	027 432 2811
Lutzville	027 217 1196
Malmesbury	022 487 1289
Montagu	023 614 1860
Moorreesberg	022 433 1848
Piketberg	022 913 2040
Porterville	022 931 2017
Riversdale	028 713 3973
Riviersonderend	028 261 1271
Robertson	023 626 4001
Saldanha	022 715 3003
Shelley Point	022 742 1906
Simonstown	021 786 1233
Somerset East	042 243 3993
Stillbaai	028 754 2625
Stutterheim	043 683 1508
Swellendam	028 514 1026
Theewaterskloof	028 840 2213
Vredendal	027 213 4957
Wellington	021 873 1919
Willowmore	044 923 1010

INDEX where to stay

HOTEL STARS

The Tourism Grading Council of South Africa is a voluntary scheme for accommodation establishments to be graded. The scheme grades establishments from one to five stars in various categories.
These are Hotel-Country House-Lodge-Guest House – Bed and Breakfast- Self-Catering.

The parting shot